SUCCESS WITH PSYCHOMETRIC TESTING

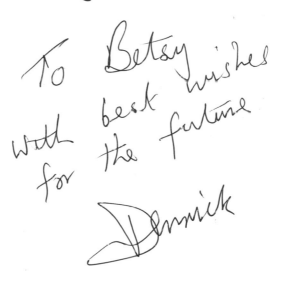

Aug 2002

To Betsy
with best wishes
for the future

Dennick

For a complete list of Management Books 2000 titles visit our web-site at http://www.mb2000.com

SUCCESS WITH PSYCHOMETRIC TESTING

Derrick White

2000

First published in 1998 by Management Books 2000 Ltd,
Cowcombe House,
Cowcombe Hill,
Chalford,
Gloucestershire GL6 8HP
Tel: 01285-760722. Fax: 01285-760708
e-mail: MB2000@compuserve.com

Printed and bound in Great Britain by Astron On-Line, Letchworth

British Library Cataloguing in Publication Data is available

ISBN 1-85252-248-8

Foreword

The chances of any individual being asked, or more likely, required to take a psychometric test at some time in their working life is extremely high. Numerous surveys report that there has been a substantial increase in the use of psychometric tests by British businesses, local government, and other organisations. Where 10% of UK companies used psychometric testing in 1980, the corresponding figure at the end of the 1990s is 85%. Where they were traditionally used for white-collar and executive recruitment, they are now being used for blue collar staff. Employers are now using psychometric tests to help with recruitment, internal promotion, career development, management development, team building, counselling, training needs analysis, succession planning, and redundancy. Some employers use psychometric tests in an attempt to determine a person's honesty. Employees and would-be employees may be invited to attend an Assessment Centre over a period of two or three days where they will be expected to carry out role playing, be interviewed, lead a team, make a presentation, and prioritise a list of activities, as well as completing one or more psychometric tests. 90% of companies with more than 4000 employees, and 50% of companies with more than 1000 employees, now use assessment centres.

One reason for the increase in the popularity of psychometric testing is that because of relatively high figures of unemployment, organisations may receive perhaps a hundred or more applicants for a single post and they use psychometric testing as a fast and cost-effective method of dealing with them. A second reason is that in comparison with other common methods used for employee recruitment, team building, career development, promotion, and so on, such as the traditional interview, taking up applicants' references, or observing potential employees, it appears that psychometric testing provides a cheaper and more standardised approach to assessing and defining individual strengths and weaknesses. Users of psychometric tests claim that they can also be used to help predict how an individual might react in certain circumstances and can provide information about individuals that would be difficult to obtain by other means. After all, they would say in defence of the use of psychometric tests, if an organisation chooses the wrong individual it can be very costly.

On the other hand, many people are very sceptical about the ability of psychometric tests to indicate unique human qualities such as personality and intelligence. It is well known that psychometric tests are not precise instruments and are open to misinterpretation – the misuse of psychometric tests has a long history. An individual may be asked to expose their innermost thoughts and beliefs – and to do so when they do not appear to be at all relevant to the situation. There have been numerous cases of staff having been dismissed after taking a psychometric test which they thought was for developmental or even promotion purposes. In 1990, eight guards working on the London Underground took their employer to court with the support of the Commission for Racial Equality, alleging that the psychometric tests they had completed were biased against applicants from ethic minorities. After using psychometric tests, Brent Council and Coventry Healthcare had to pay employees compensation for unfair dismissal, sexual, racial, and trade discrimination.

There are now hundreds of psychometric tests available, and there is growing concern with the number of untrained and unqualified individuals who develop, administer, and assess the results of these tests. Despite warnings not to do so, some organisations still select staff solely on the basis of their test results, and fail to employ qualified testers who understand what is being measured, how to interpret the results, and who recognise the legalities and ethics involved. Yet other organisations use tests to support redundancy programmes, or use handwriting analysis and astrological readings.

This book will help you understand what psychometric testing is about, and will prepare you for those occasions when you will be required to take a psychometric test. You will also learn some things about your personality and attitudes, and of the way you perceive and are perceived by other people. You will also be able to answer (or support) some of the criticisms made of psychometric testing. If you are working in an organisation which uses or is planning to use psychometric tests you will find this book invaluable and enlightening. And you will have some fun too!

Dr Howard Kahn
Heriot-Watt University, Edinburgh

To Bernice

Contents

Introduction

As a job applicant or an employee, have you ever been ushered into a room and been presented with a psychometric test? You may have been expected to respond to up to two hundred questions relating to your behaviour and attitudes.

Probably no-one explained what the test was, its purpose or how its deductions might be instrumental in deciding if you were suitable for the relevant position. The absence of intelligent communication may have made you resentful and you may have filled in the questionnaire with mounting hostility. Matters may have been made worse by the invigilator not being a psychometrician and thereby unable to answer your questions.

Knowledge is power and being kept in the dark while others make decisions about you and your responses can give you a feeling of insecurity and vulnerability. In other proficiency tests, such as a numeracy or a typing test, you understand its purpose and know instantly just how well you have done.

Psychometric tests seemed to carry the image of secrecy and created an *us* and *them* divide. Had you understood that there were clear-cut, recognised personality types and that some types predisposed the individual more favourably than others for certain types of work, you would have felt more cooperative.

As we enter a new millennium, the use of personality profiling is more the rule than the exception. A major reason for this is because much of the grindingly repetitive and physical work of the past has been replaced by machines and jobs have become much more people oriented. Service industries, sales jobs, customer handling, entertainment and recreational roles have made personality a major factor in recruitment. Despite the huge increase in its use, the level of ignorance concerning psychometrics remains high.

Having researched the subject in some depth and having applied psychometric profiling in many aspects of management from recruitment to management training, I have become a convert to the value and the remarkable accuracy of these tests. More importantly I have incorporated psychometrics into many lectures and courses on subjects such as negotiation, selling, communication skills and the principles of management. The results and the response from delegates have been very positive indeed.

Much of the early suspicion felt by many towards psychometrics was brought about by the people who were authorised or licensed to carry out such tests. These people seemed to enjoy alluding to others as *Typical X-Types, Y-Types* or *Z-Types*. Human behaviour seemed to be reduced to a range of arcane terms such as *Thinkers, Feelers, Sensors, Intuitives, Analyticals, Drivers, Supporters* and a host of other terms including animal names, single letters and even colours, all depending on the brand of test being used.

No sooner had you begun to acquire an inkling of understanding when you were told that there were 'two yous' – your *Natural self* and your *Persona*. Just as doctors and lawyers could use language like a fortress, ensuring no unwelcome outsider could penetrate their hallowed ground, so it seemed with the psychometrician.

Worse, one could develop the uncomfortable feeling that some of the people involved in the field did not fully understand their subject. The mysterious and often lengthy questionnaires they used never seemed to be scrutinised by anything so ordinary as the human eye or brain. No, the answers were fed into a state of the art computer to be analysed by the most advanced software package, all adding to the mystique.

In a recruitment situation, an applicant might be judged not suitable on the advice of a computer print-out. When challenged as to why, the reply could be side-stepped by affording the computer programme a reverence verging on infallibility, rather than facing an in-depth discussion which the recruiter might be ill-equipped to handle.

Many managers argued that all they needed was half an hour in the pub with someone and they could make a sound decision as to whether that person was suitable for whatever position was available. Moreover, they could decide how well that person would fit into a department. I support that view but I have learned to understand and value psychometric profiling as a highly accurate method of reaching the same deduction. It is a tool and in some circumstances it is indispensable. This book's objective is to show how valuable it can be in many aspects of human exchange such as, in business:

- recruitment
- team building – balanced teams and focused teams
- promotion and job changes
- selling – adapting to type
- negotiation
- understanding company cultures
- understanding 'blind spots'
- understanding how stress can develop

or in one's personal life:

- understanding ourselves
  understanding personal relationships
- understanding our children
- knowing why we feel uncomfortable with some individuals
- learning to differentiate between *natural self* and *persona*
- why great and not-so-great minds think alike

So, whether you are one of the psychometric faithful or a sceptic let us look at the principles of psychometric profiling and how they can benefit you.

1

What Does Psychometric Mean?

We use terms to describe personality on a daily basis. We call people extrovert and introvert, hot-blooded and cold-blooded. We all know the strong, silent type and the person who is very 'touchy-feely'. You've met the green, caring earth-mother and the real bossy-boots. You've worked hard with the party guest where conversation was like drawing teeth and you've silently prayed that the deafening life and soul of the party would choke on a prawn cracker.

All that psychometric tests do is quantify what one's personality preferences are. The word *meter* means measure and *psyche* means mind or soul. So a psychometric test is simply one which measures your mind or, more precisely, your attitudes. IQ tests measure your intelligence while literacy and numeracy tests measure your ability to express your thoughts in writing and to reason arithmetically.

Psychometric types are also known as *Four Quadrant Behaviour* (4QB). The advantage of this term is that it is self-explanatory. Human behaviour is categorised into four base types. Subtypes of eight, sixteen, thirty-two and beyond can be identified. A simple analogy is seeing four primary colours on a palette. By mixing different concentrations of each, the number of variations of colour is virtually infinite. However we only need to concentrate on the four primary types in 4QB to develop a working knowledge of the subject.

THE ORIGINS OF 4QB

When were these four types first identified and by whom?

We tend to associate psychology with bearded Swiss analysts in white coats and with quaint guttural accents. Switzerland certainly contributed more than most, but the original Four Quadrants were identified in ancient Greece by the father of modern medicine, Hippocrates (b.460 BC), after whom the oath taken by doctors was named.

He and his colleagues noted that although the symptoms of common complaints did not vary a great deal, the manner with which the patients described them varied quite distinctly.

Type One

A type one patient might describe an abdominal pain as,

Got this pain in the gut, Doc. Damn nuisance. I'm sure it's nothing. Wouldn't bother you normally but it was the wife's idea that I came. Probably a bit of wind. Just give me a pill or whatever and I'll be off.

Type Two

The type two individual is different and would put it thus,

Hi Doc! How're you. Ages since I've seen you. Keeping busy? Like your new receptionist, great girl, warm, friendly, makes you feel glad you came. How am I? Oh fine, just a bit of a stomach pain. Might be something to do with the double helping of moussaka and the half dozen bottles of retsina. It was worth it though – what a night!

Type Three

The type three character was quite distinct again.

Hello Doctor. How are you? And your wife Helen and little Ariadne? What age is she now? Really! How was your holiday in the Cyclades? That's good. Oh me? Well, I have this pain in the tummy. Seems identical to the one my sister Hermione had. She was quite distressed. In bed for a week she was. You gave her some purgative. Poor thing, she was never off the loo. She's better now, bless her, got her appetite and her colour back. Her husband Oedipus was even worse but, between you and me Doctor, he was always a bit precious, a real mother's boy.

Type Four

Finally, the type four patient is again distinctly individual.

Doctor, I have a pain in the left lower abdomen. Began at 3am on Saturday and by midday it had developed from dull to acute. Temperature has been constant at 98.7 which is point three above my normal. Passing of urine normal but bowel movements have decreased from once in twenty-four hours to once in thirty-six. Appetite is suppressed, otherwise no observable symptoms.

THE FOUR HUMOURS

Hippocrates had identified four distinct types. He called them *The Four Humours* (explained in just a moment).

- **Type One**
  was abrupt, businesslike, assertive, no fuss, straight to the point. Here's the problem. Do something. Get on with it. Hippocrates gave this type the name *Choleric*.

19

- **Type Two**
  was sunny, cheerful, expressive, friendly, outgoing, enjoyed life and liked to party. These Hippocrates called *Sanguine*.

- **Type Three**
  was caring, intimate, a people person, concerned about relationships and chatty. These he identified as *Phlegmatic*.

- **Type Four**
  appeared cool, detached, analytical, factual and unemotional. These were given the name *Melancholic*.

Why such names? These early doctors believed that there was a relationship between the various fluids of the body and the nature of the individual.

Choleric was derived from the word 'choler', the Greek for bile. People affected by the bile tended to be assertive, irascible, abrupt, abrasive and impatient. Bile or bilious is still used in everyday speech to denote ill-humour.

Sanguines were said to be influenced by the blood. The Hippocratic associations are still used in terms such as red-blooded or hot-blooded to describe someone who is outgoing, demonstrative and who lives life to the full. To be quite sanguine about an idea is to be happy with it.

Phlegmatic, as you might have guessed is linked with phlegm. People with this association were said to be calm, which remains its meaning. The psychometric disposition is broader, meaning not only calm but caring, concerned with relationships and preferring harmony to assertion.

Melancholic has come to mean sad and dejected. The psychometric meaning is not so blue. The word, derived from black bile (Greek 'melas' for black + bile) in 4QB describes a type who is analytical, pensive, detached and cool.

Hippocrates used the collective, descriptive term **The Four Humours**. This seems quite consistent as we regularly ask questions such as, 'What sort of humour is he in?'

Although 'humour' is generally associated with fun, its original meaning from the Latin is 'to be moist' and most dictionaries define humour as *a fluid of the animal body* as well as the usual 'sense of humour' meanings. So, in two and a half millennia, Hippocrates' summary or measure of the human psyche has changed very little indeed. His Four Humours are now identified by psychometricians as Four Quadrant Behaviour. While we all now use the term 4QB, Hippocrates' terminology has stood the test of time and is as clearly descriptive now as it was then.

A general maxim in the field of training is, *If you can't explain it to a five-year-old, you can't explain it.* If I had to explain psychometric types to a group of five-year-olds, Hippocrates' Four Humours would be my choice

4 **Melancholic**	**1** **Choleric**
3 **Phlegmatic**	**2** **Sanguine**

Fig 1. The Four Quadrants/Humours

BUT I THINK KNEW ABOUT 4QB ALL ALONG

Whenever a philosophy or theorem is explained clearly, we tend to be less impressed than we might be because deep within us we always knew the inherent truth of the theory. We don't need Isaac Newton to tell us that a rubber ball dropped from a height of one metre will not bounce as high as one dropped from ten metres. However we do need his calculations to work out precisely the rate of acceleration of a falling object.

A schoolboy who was hopeless at geometry and physics can develop into a world-class snooker player, calculating by sheer instinct the forces, speed and angles of shots of breathtaking complexity.

When first introduced to Maslow's *Hierarchy of Needs*, you could be forgiven for finding it simplistic and facile. In essence, Maslow expounded that humans had needs, wants and aspirations which formed a hierarchy, shown normally in the form of a pyramid, (Fig.2).

At the bottom level is simple survival and staying alive (food and drink). When that need is met, we move up a level. The next need is for security (safe cave or home), followed by the need for love and affection (spouse, family). These satisfied, we seek recognition or status and finally we want to be great, the big cheese, the VIP. Obvious really, we all understand that. But it took Maslow to identify the hierarchy so clearly and define each level.

MASLOW AS A REFERENCE POINT

Simplistic as it may be, Maslow's hierarchy has been universally accepted and its principles are applied in many ways. It can determine a management strategy. Sales driven organisations know that an award ceremony at a prestigious venue will do more to motivate a salesperson than a pay rise. How many men (it's nearly always the men) have changed companies through the blandishment of a superior motor car. Daily we are bombarded by advertising which is Maslow inspired. Car advertisements alone incorporate every level. Survival and security – air bags, ABS braking, crumple zones. Belonging, love – look at the Clio ads where Nicole and Papa are in constant pursuit of nookie liaisons. Not a mention of performance, safety or economy – just a cuddly aura. The smarter marques of cars are sold unashamedly on the strengths of Maslow's clearly identified need for status.

Fig 2

WHAT'S MASLOW GOT TO DO WITH 4QB

It's a fair question and the answer is twofold.

First, we might look upon Maslow's levels as obvious, like gravity, but it is only when the consistency and power of these principles are realised that we can see how profound they are. So with 4QB (Fig.1). We always knew that some people were bossy, irascible, impatient and forceful (choleric), while others were the diametric opposite (phlegmatic) – calm, caring, passive and concerned about relationships. The other two humours are also opposites. We've all met the sanguines – outgoing, talkative, sunny and noisy. Equally we recognise their opposite or *blind spot*, the melancholic – cool, detached, contemplative, analytical and slow to express emotion. So we knew about 4QB all along. Maybe in a cognitive sense we did, but it took Hippocrates to identify the four distinct types. Those who followed on in the twentieth century, most notably Carl Gustav Jung, only gave a more scientific substance to the ancient Greek's seminal and wholly accurate observations.

Second, there is a correlation between the levels of Maslow's pyramid and 4QB, in that each of the four types would be influenced by the different levels of the hierarchy. For example the VIP and STATUS levels are more likely to relate to the cholerics and sanguines whereas the BELONGING & LOVE element could have broader appeal to the phlegmatics.

SUCCESSES OF APPLIED MASLOW

You're never alone with a Strand

One of the greatest examples of applied Maslow was with Embassy cigarettes. The Embassy started life as the Strand. The slogan was *You're never alone with a Strand* and the ad featured a Sinatra lookalike all alone by the Thames, lighting a Strand on a murky evening. Catchy idea and good visuals but the Strand bombed. Precisely the same cigarette was repackaged as

Embassy, but this time the image was of people at a party having a wonderful time and offering each other an Embassy. The message was changed from an image of loneliness to one of togetherness and, in the popular cliché, the rest is history; Embassy went on to be the No 1 brand in the UK.

Takes your breath away

Similarly, when Smirnoff vodka was first marketed in the US, various angles were tried from its exoticness to its purity but sales never took off. It was only when the winning idea of social acceptability was employed that sales figures began to rocket. The slogan was *It takes your breath away* and the message was clear – a few drinks at lunchtime or on the way home will not result in offensive boozey breath.

QUESTIONS

Q. Can you illustrate 4QB using four well known figures?

A. You can identify the qualities in famous people but there is a risk in assuming that it is a one hundred per cent accurate representation. Public people often have public faces and without a thorough psychometric test, there is room for error. However, insofar as 4QB can be identified, the choleric – assertive, bossy and impatient – was displayed very much by Margaret Thatcher. Bill Clinton conveys very much the sanguine – smiling, chatty, friendly and expressive. Jimmy Carter showed most of the characteristics of the phlegmatic – caring, sincere, unaggressive and seeking harmony. The melancholic traits were seen very much in Richard Nixon – detached, wary, introspective and suspicious.

Q. Do companies have quadrant preferences for different jobs?

A. It depends very much on the culture of the company and the nature of the service it provides. In general, 4QB represents four qualities:

1. Assertiveness
2. Buoyancy
3. A caring approach
4. An analytical approach

so companies will probably prefer to fill positions as follows:

1. Managers, team leaders, (sales – depending on company culture)
2. Team leaders and those in PR, promotional activities or reception
3. People working in personnel, customer handling or reception
4. Engineers, scientists, chemists, accountants

2

Self Analysis

ESTABLISH YOUR OWN QUADRANT

Before proceeding any further into psychometric types and how they interact with one another, pause for a few minutes and complete your own personal questionnaire (Fig.3.) to ascertain which *Humour* or *Quadrant* type you fit most. It is important to do this now because later we are going to look at the strengths and weaknesses of each type in some detail. If you examine each type before you complete the questionnaire, you could adopt a prejudice for or against a particular quadrant and as a consequence you might answer the questions in a less than natural and spontaneous way.

So here is what to do. In Fig 3, there are twenty groups of statements. In each group, there are four statements relating to normal human behaviour. One of these statements is most like you and one of them is least like you. Tick one Most box and tick one Least box. For example, in group one, the four examples of human behaviour are,

M L
☐ ☐   **Considerate of others**
☐ ☐   **Withdrawn and reflective**

☐ ☐   **Determined and forceful**
☐ ☐   **Outgoing and boisterous**

You may decide that the fourth statement is most like you and that the second statement is least like you. Just tick statement four under M and statement two under L. With some of the statements you may find that none of them is very like you or very unlike you. This is not uncommon. However, one statement will be the closest to being like you and one will be closest to being most unlike you. Choose one of each. Respond to the groups as spontaneously and quickly as you reasonably can. Don't dwell too long on the statements as you may produce a distorted picture. If you find you simply cannot decide on a specific group, skip it. There are twenty groups of statements and nineteen or even eighteen answered accurately will still give a true representation of your type in a 4QB connotation.

    Complete the 'Most Like You / Least Like You' questionnaire in Fig 3. Then go to Fig 4 and total the number of each of the four humours or quadrants with which you identify most. Then do the same for the least. Now take some paper and write two columns thus,

MOST	LEAST
D =	**D** =
I =	**I** =
S =	**S** =
C =	**C** =

Fig 3. Most like you / least like you questionnaire
(M = most like you, L = least like you; tick just one of each)

	M	L	
1.	❑	❑	**Considerate of others**
	❑	❑	**Withdrawn and reflective**
	❑	❑	**Determined and forceful**
	❑	❑	**Outgoing and boisterous**
2.	❑	❑	**Demanding, rapid**
	❑	❑	**Helpful, caring**
	❑	❑	**Charming, talkative**
	❑	❑	**Perfectionist**
3.	❑	❑	**Dynamic, challenging**
	❑	❑	**Incisive, must be right**
	❑	❑	**Emotional, friendly**
	❑	❑	**Painstaking, quiet**
4.	❑	❑	**Thoughtful, formal**
	❑	❑	**Encouraging, accepting**
	❑	❑	**Assertive, driving**
	❑	❑	**Life and soul of party**
5.	❑	❑	**Unassuming, kindly**
	❑	❑	**Flamboyant, excitable**
	❑	❑	**Abrasive, decisive**
	❑	❑	**Distant, slow to intimacy**

6.   **M**   **L**

- ❑   ❑   Cooperative, agreeable
- ❑   ❑   Stubborn, combative
- ❑   ❑   Fun-loving, restless
- ❑   ❑   Logical, unexcitable

7.   **M**   **L**

- ❑   ❑   Sticks to principles
- ❑   ❑   Analytical, unemotional
- ❑   ❑   Overbearing. leader
- ❑   ❑   Easily distracted, giddy

8.   **M**   **L**

- ❑   ❑   Sincere, trustworthy
- ❑   ❑   Brave, unafraid
- ❑   ❑   Undemonstrative, resigned
- ❑   ❑   Good mixer, enjoys company

9.   **M**   **L**

- ❑   ❑   Suspicious, wary
- ❑   ❑   Generous, willing to share
- ❑   ❑   Persuasive, convincing
- ❑   ❑   Bombastic, task-driven

10.   **M**   **L**

- ❑   ❑   No self-doubt, forceful
- ❑   ❑   Soft-spoken, formal
- ❑   ❑   Articulate, smooth talker
- ❑   ❑   Accommodating, agreeable

11.   **M**   **L**

- ❑   ❑   Sociable, enjoy others' company
- ❑   ❑   Tolerant and patient
- ❑   ❑   Self-reliant and strong
- ❑   ❑   Accurate and correct

	M	L	
12.			
	❑	❑	**Spontaneous, impulsive**
	❑	❑	**Trusting, loyal**
	❑	❑	**Thorough and detailed**
	❑	❑	**Strong-minded, pushy**
13.			
	❑	❑	**Pedantic, deliberate**
	❑	❑	**Responsive, affectionate**
	❑	❑	**Authoritative, bossy**
	❑	❑	**Demonstrative, indiscreet**
14.			
	❑	❑	**Irrational, challenging**
	❑	❑	**Passive, soothing**
	❑	❑	**Results driven**
	❑	❑	**Methodical, disciplined**
15.			
	❑	❑	**Controlling, competitive**
	❑	❑	**Questioning, self-controlled**
	❑	❑	**Disorganised, unstructured**
	❑	❑	**Loyal, supporting**
16.			
	❑	❑	**Unyielding, argumentative**
	❑	❑	**Slow to anger, peacemaker**
	❑	❑	**Cool, dutiful**
	❑	❑	**Easily distracted, let's party**
17.			
	❑	❑	**Warm, friendly**
	❑	❑	**Win at all costs, do it my way**
	❑	❑	**Detached, studious**
	❑	❑	**Extrovert, noisy**

18. M   L
  ❑ ❑   **Exuberant, loud**
  ❑ ❑   **Confrontational**
  ❑ ❑   **Willing to help and listen**
  ❑ ❑   **Cautious, quiet**

19. M   L
  ❑ ❑   **Lenient, not overstrict**
  ❑ ❑   **Reserved, unforthcoming**
  ❑ ❑   **Original, individualistic**
  ❑ ❑   **Sociable, cheerful**

20. M   L
  ❑ ❑   **Good-natured, pleasing**
  ❑ ❑   **Inspiring, optimistic**
  ❑ ❑   **Tough-minded, gutsy**
  ❑ ❑   **Calculating, observant**

Fig 4. Interpretation table

Your answers all correspond to the letters D, I, S or C listed below (which will be explained later). Mark your **MOST LIKE YOU** first with an M then your **LEAST LIKE YOU** with an L:

1.	Considerate of others	S
	Withdrawn and reflective	C
	Determined and forceful	D
	Outgoing and boisterous	I
2.	Demanding, rapid	D
	Helpful, caring	S
	Charming, talkative	I
	Perfectionist	C
3.	Dynamic, challenging	I
	Incisive, must be right	D
	Emotional, friendly	S
	Painstaking, quiet	C
4.	Thoughtful, formal	C
	Encouraging, accepting	S
	Assertive, driving	D
	Life and soul of party	I
5.	Unassuming, kindly	S
	Flamboyant, excitable	I
	Abrasive, decisive	D
	Distant, slow to intimacy	C
6.	Cooperative, agreeable	S
	Stubborn, combative	D
	Fun-loving, restless	I
	Logical, unexcitable	C

7.	Sticks to principles	S
	Analytical, unemotional	C
	Overbearing. leader	D
	Easily distracted, giddy	I

8.	Sincere, trustworthy	S
	Brave, unafraid	C
	Undemonstrative, resigned	D
	Good mixer, enjoys company	I

9.	Suspicious, wary	C
	Generous, willing to share	S
	Persuasive, convincing	I
	Bombastic, task-driven	D

10.	No self-doubt, forceful	D
	Soft-spoken, formal	C
	Articulate, smooth talker	I
	Accommodating, agreeable	S

11.	Sociable, enjoy others' company	I
	Tolerant and patient	S
	Self-reliant and strong	D
	Accurate and corrrect	C

12.	Spontaneous, impulsive	I
	Trusting, loyal	S
	Thorough and detailed	C
	Strong-minded, pushy	D

13.	Pedantic, deliberate	C
	Responsive, affectionate	S
	Authoritative, bossy	D
	Demonstrative, indiscreet	I

14.	Irrational, challenging	I
	Passive, soothing	S
	Results driven	D
	Methodical, disciplined	C

15.	Controlling, competitive	D
	Questioning, self-controlled	C
	Disorganised, unstructured	I
	Loyal, supporting	S

16.	Unyielding, argumentative	D
	Slow to anger, peacemaker	S
	Cool, dutiful	C
	Easily distracted, let's party	I

17.	Warm, friendly	S
	Win at all costs, do it my way	D
	Detached, studious	C
	Extrovert, noisy	I

18.	Exuberant, loud	S
	Confrontational	D
	Willing to help and listen	C
	Cautious, quiet	I

19.	Lenient, not overstrict	S
	Reserved, unforthcoming	C
	Original, individualistic	D
	Sociable, cheerful	I

20.	Good-natured, pleasing	S
	Inspiring, optimistic	I
	Tough-minded, gutsy	D
	Calculating, observant	C

WHY DISC ?

Although Hippocrates' original terms for The Four Humours are in many ways preferable, it is a bit of a mouthful to refer constantly to Cholerics, Sanguines, Phlegmatics and Melancholics. So for ease of use, a single letter denoting each character trait makes for easier reference. Why DISC? There are several organisations which practise in the field of psychometric testing. Though all of them adhere to the same fundamental principles, several have developed their own terminology, which we shall look at in more detail in Chapter 3. The most commonly used of all the descriptions to identify the four quadrants is DISC. This equates with Hippocrates as follows:

Choleric ....**Dominant or Driving**
Sanguine ....**Inspiring or Influencing**
Phlegmatic ....**Supporting or Steadfast**
Melancholic ....**Coordinating or Compliant**

An alternative which I have used in the past is to keep the initial letters (CSPM) of Hippocrates' Four Humours using **Combative, Sunny, Passive** and **Meticulous,** but as a rule I find it beneficial, for obvious reasons, to share a common language with other psychometricians and the most common language for this purpose is DISC. So rather than confuse the reader who may have to translate from one language to another, DISC will be used throughout.

Dominant, Inspiring, Supportive and Coordinating are effective terms to describe 4QB. The four quadrants are to be explored in some depth but a brief typification is found on pages 51 and 52.

Right, so you've counted up your score and you might for example find the results look like this:

MOST	LEAST
D = 2	D = 9
I = 5	I = 4
S = 9	S = 2
C = 4	C = 5

Plot these totals on two graphs as in Fig 5.

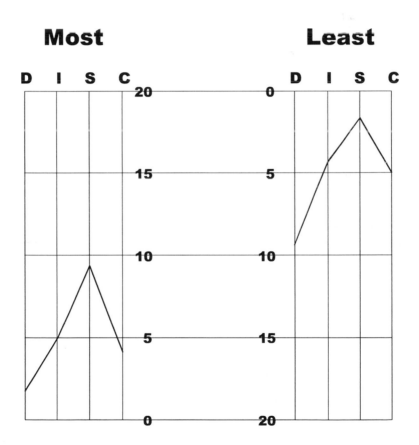

Fig 5

In order to obtain a visual correlation between the two graphs, the Least graph is inverted. If you identified with S the most, it is logical that you might reject S the least, therefore, if plotted on the same ascending configuration of zero-to-twenty, the second picture would be a diametric opposite of the first.

We'll take a look at the significance of Most and Least in a moment, but assuming there was no distinction between the two, the graphs show a clear pattern. The predominant quadrant is **S** – Supporting, sympathetic, caring. (Phlegmatic) and the least is **D** – Dominant, driving, assertive. (Choleric).

The remaining two, **I** for inspiring and innovative (Sanguine) with **C** for coordinating and calculating (Melancholic) are present in roughly equal amounts somewhere in the middle.

READING THE GRAPH

The benefit of a graph is that it gives an instant visual representation of the 4QB make-up of an individual. The graph in Fig 5 is a thumbnail sketch of someone we'll call Chris. Using the most simplistic analysis, Chris is a High-S whose preference is to support, to be sympathetic, to be caring, considerate and preferring harmony and cooperation in dealings with others. Chris's next strongest preference is I for Inspiring. The Inspiring quadrant is buoyant, happy, motivational, talkative and sunny, so Chris quite likes to party and is probably a very good mixer being both sympathetic and sunny. Chris has a reasonable measure of the C quadrant which is identified with analytical thought, concentration, precision, thoroughness and an affinity for detail. Chris's weakest or least pronounced preference is D, which indicates that Chris prefers not to be authoritative, assertive, abrupt, impatient and bossy. If Chris were a manager or team leader as a High-S, Low-D, he would prefer to lead through harmony and cooperation rather than by assertion or with a dictatorial style.

Chris's analysis is deliberately presented in the least complicated manner. Psychometric profiling can become quite deep but the clarity of this example will help form the basis of greater understanding in future chapters.

CASE STUDIES

The Brilliant Trainer

An English based consultancy was seeking high quality trainers. One CV particularly impressed the company. The applicant, Thomas, had excelled at all stages of education, finally taking a degree course at the Harvard Law School. Thomas was offered the position and very soon was asked to take on a training project for a major client. He researched the client's history, staffing, needs and potential. The course material Thomas put together was thorough, detailed and clearly the product of high academic ability. The duration of the course was a week and the venue a country hotel with fine amenities and a relaxed atmosphere. The delegates were twelve of the client company's key people.

By day two, there were mutterings of discontent. At the end of day three, word was getting back to the client office that all was not well. Day four saw two absences and day five had to finish early.

The delegates found the course too heavy, arid and boring. Though acknowledging the trainer's IQ, they found Thomas distant, unhelpful and rather impatient. Had a psychometric test been used, it would have been established that Thomas was a High-C (cool, detached, analytical). So, while the course material reflected great intellectual effort, the trainer lacked those vital skills of warmth, empathy, humour and expressiveness, now known as communication skills. The trainer was indeed brilliant but personal brilliance is not sufficient in a classroom situation. Also, outside the classroom, delegates wanted to relax, have a drink and enjoy themselves, while the High-C trainer was content to review the course material.

Personnel jobs are more than being good with people

The interview panel all took to Alan. They liked his friendly, open, cheery and enthusiastic manner. Alan was offered the vacancy in Personnel. Initially his popularity grew. Everybody liked the new person in Personnel who had a friendly word for everyone and enjoyed a laugh and a joke. After some time the honeymoon period waned and some of the staff's relationship with Alan began to sour. Critical words like 'insincere' and 'uncaring' could be heard. The problem was that Alan was a very much a High-I, extrovert, noisy and the life and soul of the party. When dealing with personnel problems, Alan could be inspiring and cheery but lacked the real concern of the High-S who is noted for loyalty, sincerity and caring qualities. Neither did Alan have the attention to detail of the High-C who, though less warm, would keep thorough personnel records and be accurate with dates, family details, illnesses and the many factors which affect staff. One other important factor – confidentiality is an essential component of the personnel professional's make-up. The High-I is by nature gregarious and discretion may not be as pronounced as it should be in the role. Buoyancy is a good quality in personnel but too much of it, to the exclusion of other valuable qualities, is a risk.

QUESTIONS

Q. I'm very much a C but I'd like to go into selling. Should I try?

A. Selling is seen very much as an I skill. Certainly, if you wished to be a Del Boy selling crockery or household goods from a market stall, your C nature might find it difficult. But there are many products and services being sold very successfully by Cs, such as financial services, computer hardware and software, office equipment, motor cars – in fact any product or service which interests you. If you are interested in what you sell, that interest will be transmitted to the buyer whatever quadrant you present from. Do remember that selling is all about making contacts – numbers and dogged hard work – not just making flashy presentations.

Q. Why are there different psychometric tests?

A. The major commercial players are listed elsewhere. In essence they are all based on 4QB but each quadrant has quite lengthy descriptions within it. So one quadrant might have dozens of adjectives which accurately describe the behaviour associated with it. Some companies do not just settle for the broad brush approach of the four preferences, they want to gauge some of the sub-definitions as well. For example the Occupational Personality Questionnaire (OPQ) subdefines thirty personality scales including the adjectives: independent, modest, democratic, conscientious, practical, artistic, emotional control and competitive. Thereby they can fine-tune a personality reading. However, all thirty of the personality factors could each be placed in one of four trays marked D, I, S or C. Some of them could be placed in more than one tray. Modest for example could be a descriptive term for S or C, so OPQ's strength is its ability to focus-in and fine-tune.

3

Psychometrics Today

Hippocrates' Four Humours were the only yardstick for psychometric evaluation until the 1920s. In 1921 Carl Gustav Jung published *Psychological Types* and in 1928 Dr William Marston wrote *The Emotions of Normal People* linking his work with the research already carried out by Jung. The four Hippocratic prototypes remained, but Jung added a further division across all four, *Extrovert* and *Introvert*, making eight distinct types in all. Jung's work was consolidated by his associate, Dr Jolande Jacobi, and was published by her in 1942 with the title *The Psychology of C. G. Jung*.

UNDERSTANDING JUNG'S WHEEL

Jung's eight classic personality types were expressed in the form of a circle or wheel. In essence, Jung had taken the four Hippocratic quadrants of ninety degree sectors and divided them into eight sectors of forty-five degrees. Jung discarded Hippocrates' Humours or fluids and although the words Choleric, Sanguine, Phlegmatic and Melancholic remain in common usage, psychologists and all the psychometric testing companies prefer to use the Jungian terms. In recognition of this, we'll take a look at the professional terminology because your interest in psychometrics is guaranteed to grow and if you discuss the subject with others similarly interested, these are the terms they will use. We use the words Northerners, Southerners, Easterners and Westerners often to describe an origin or type. In England, the terms Northerner and Southerner express a judgemental view or prejudice. In Scotland there are divisions between Highlander and Lowlander or East Coast types and West Coast types. In the US, all four points convey a separate image. Jung mapped out his four base types like compass points and he called them THINKERS, FEELERS, SENSORS and INTUITIVES.

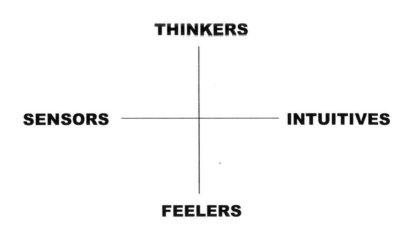

Fig 6

THINKERS

Rather than define the type in Jungian terms, consider a child. This child can sit quietly absorbed with some toy, object or book. The caring parent observes the child ten minutes later, still apparently content and happy. The parent asks the child if everything is okay. 'Aha', affirms the child calmly. The THINKER's behaviour is to perceive the world by observation.

FEELERS

Feelers, on the other hand just have to be touching and exploring everything. This kid is into cupboards, drawers, desks, boxes – you name it. The resultant mess is simply the by-product of an exploratory nature.

The behaviour of adult THINKERS and FEELERS will naturally differ from the obvious traits in children. Take someone who appears very distressed. The THINKER will want to know what happened. An accident? How did it happen? Where? When? – factual, objective, analytical. Not unsympathetic, simply fact-oriented with a priority to gain correct information.

The FEELER's first reaction would be to soothe, to put an arm round the upset person, to comfort, then later check out the facts.

In Fig 6, if THINKER is scaled at 1 and FEELER at 10, with the intersection at 5, award yourself a mark – where do you place yourself along this line?

SENSORS AND INTUITIVES

SENSORS and INTUITIVES have similar character divisions but are distinct types. One way to describe these two is as two interviewers. The SENSOR by definition needs to check everything out with all five senses. She is the one who will read the

CV, check the references, confirm that the educational qualifications are correct, look for discrepancies in the dates of previous jobs and so on. She will also, more than likely, telephone previous employers or referees for comment. After the interview, she turns to the INTUITIVE and asks, 'What did you think?'

The INTUITIVE replies, 'No, I don't feel he is suitable'. This annoys the SENSOR who demands, 'Why ever not? You haven't even read the CV, nor looked at the references!' The INTUITIVE answers, 'There was just something about him I didn't like'

You know the situation. An apparently good track record conflicting with a gut feeling. The police use a combination of these two types in investigations. One has a great aptitude for acquiring and absorbing facts while the other has a keen ability to observe demeanour and aura. Ideally they should arrive at the same conclusion via different routes but these two types can conflict in their deductions and may never be quite happy with the other's modus operandi.

PLACE YOURSELF ON JUNG's CIRCLE.

Your personal disposition will lie somewhere along the SENSOR INTUITIVE line. Using the 1 to 10 scale, award yourself another mark. Together with the first one you made, this should place you in one of the four quadrants which should correspond with the result of the questionnaire you completed in Chapter 2.

Jung therefore produced four 'compass' points which in turn produce four distinct quadrants the North East, South East, South West and North West which conform graphically to the Hippocratic quadrants. and to the Ancient Greek's four humours. Take the NW quadrant.

Someone who is halfway between a **Sensor** and a **Thinker** prefers facts, detail, analytical thought and objectivity – Hippocrates' classic **Melancholic** or **C Type**. Likewise the diametric opposite, people in the quadrant bounded by **Intuitives** and **Feelers** will be expressive, outgoing and impulsive. They'll dislike long scientific analysis and orthodox systems – the classic **Sanguine** or **I Type**.

So although Jung approached the identification of the four types from a psychological premise and Hippocrates chose a physiological root using body fluids, they both arrived at the same four types. So Ancient Greek and modern Swiss would have found common ground in The Four Humours and 4QB.

Jung developed a science around psychological types and he lectured all over the world until his death in 1961 at the age of eighty-six. One of Jung's developments was to add the two further divisions of **Extrovert** and **Introvert** thus producing eight distinct types. The Extrovert he placed on the East side of the wheel and the Introvert on the West side.

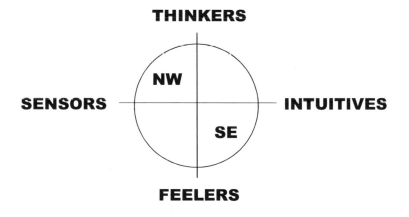

Fig 7

These eight types are generally expressed by using the initial letter of each of the descriptive terms. (As both **Introvert** and **Intuitive** begin with I, the descriptive initial for Intuitive is always expressed as an N.) So Jung's eight types are codified as:

INF	INTROVERT INTUITIVE FEELER
ISF	INTROVERT SENSING FEELER
IST	INTROVERT SENSING THINKER
INT	INTROVERT INTUITIVE THINKER
EST	EXTROVERT SENSING THINKER
ENT	EXTROVERT INTUITIVE THINKER
ENF	EXTROVERT INTUITIVE FEELER
ESF	EXTROVERT SENSING FEELER

I CAN'T REMEMBER ALL THOSE AWKWARD PHRASES.

There is no need to. For the remainder of this book only the 4QB Types D,I,S and C (NE, SE, SW and NW) will be used. Jung's terms are only included in deference to him as the world's leading figure in the development of psychological typology.

MAIN COMMERCIAL PLAYERS.

It is useful to know who the main commercial players are in the field of psychometric testing. If you have completed a personality test, it is almost a certainty that the author/originator of the test will have been one of the following:

Belbin
Insights International

> **Myers-Briggs**
> **Saville & Holdsworth (OPQ)**
> **Thomas International**
> **Wilson Learning**
> **16PF**
> **Whetstone Training**
> **Team Management Systems (Margerison & McCann)**

All these companies and others not included, vary in their approach to the test and in their analysis of the outcome. Some use as few as two dozen questions while others use over two hundred. Some use Jung's letter indicators (INT, ESF etc), some use descriptive terms which vary from system to system, i.e. Motivator, Inspirer, Reporter, Advisor, Helper, Controller and a host of others). Still others use animals (Owl for the analytical C-Type or Porpoise for the expressive I-Type). **Myers-Briggs** embellished Jung's eight types with the suffixes J and P for Judging and Perceiving producing a combination such as INTP or INTJ. The two extra divisions (which will remain unexplored) now produce sixteen psychological types. Currently in the UK, two of the most commonly used psychological tests are **OPQ** (Occupational Personality Questionnaire) and **16PF** (Sixteen Personality Factor Questionnaire). OPQ's questionnaires measure from thirty human characteristics down to six, while 16PF measures, as the name suggests, sixteen. All are highly effective but in-depth analysis of each is not necessary for the purposes of this book or for greater understanding of everyday inter-personal communication.

DISC

In commercial use the most common abbreviation for the four quadrants is DISC. You will hear psychometricians talk of a DISC-based system. This is not an allusion to a floppy disc but is a reference to the four elements of **4QB** – Dominant or Driving, Inspiring or Influencing, Steadfast or Supporting and

Coordinating or Compliant. Staff in personnel departments will refer to people for example as High-D, High-S or Low-I, Low-C. Another method of expressing **4QB** is **DEAA** – Drivers, Expressives, Amiables, Analyticals (Wilson Learning). Yet another is ABCD – Assertive, Buoyant, Caring, Detached (Insights International).

Compare the three and in terms of human behaviour you could not get a cigarette paper between them.

D.I.S.C. =   **Dominance**
                       Influence
                       Steadfastness
                       Compliance

A.B.C.D. =   **Assertive**
                       Buoyant
                       Caring/Calming
                       Detached

D.E.A.A. =   **Driving**
                       Expressive
                       Amiable
                       Analytical

Throw in Hippocrates' Four Humours and the picture is complete:

Four humours =   **Choleric**
                       Sanguine
                       Phlegmatic
                       Melancholic

You may be told one system is superior to another. They are all inherently sound but it depends on the objective. The broad-brush approach might be perfectly adequate for general recruitment but in appointing someone to a sensitive and responsible position it might be necessary to take specific personality factors and weigh them individually.

QUADRANTS AS GIFTS

One absolute rule in the study of psychometrics is that each quadrant should be seen as a gift. Some psychometricians use the term *preferences*. Like being left-handed or right-handed, there is no innate superiority in either, they are simply preferences. Whether you are D, I, S or C, that is your preference or gift. That is the way you are and your specific behavioural type is invaluable to humanity. We'll look at Team Building later but it is worth stressing now that in some corporations the company culture might be High-C or High-D and if you don't belong to that quadrant you might feel your face did not fit and that you were the square peg. You may even try to alter your natural personality to conform to the dominant type culture.

GOOD DAYS AND BAD DAYS

While each of the quadrants should be seen as a gift, it is worth remembering that each type has its strengths and its weaknesses. In the table below can be seen clear advantages in each type and for balance, the disadvantages.

	STRENGTHS (*Good Day*)	**WEAKNESSES** (*Bad Day*)
High-D	Assertive	Aggressive
	Decisive	Impatient
	Direct	Insensitive
	Waffle-free	Abrupt
	Demanding	Poor Listener

High-I	Buoyant	Interrupting
	Ebullient	Irritating
	Friendly	Keen to be liked
	Creative	Fickle
	Spontaneous	Lacking depth
High-S	Good listener	Negative
	Amiable	Fence-Sitter
	Balanced	Indecisive
	People-oriented	Lacks focus
	Compassionate	Passive
High-C	Thorough	Slow to respond
	Good with details	Bad with people
	Accurate	Too formal
	Objective	Ignores feelings
	Cool and detached	Uncommunicative

WHY THE 'MOST & LEAST' LIKE YOU

A thorough psychometric test will include these two factors. Sometimes the headings are *How You See Yourself* and *How Others See You*. However obtained, they are simply two reflections of you. Rather like two mirrors at two different angles reflecting two separate profiles. In Jungian terms one is your natural self and the other is your persona (Latin – *player's mask*), also known as your *Adapted Style*. The Least like you characteristics are generally the easiest to fill in. We skim down them fairly quickly – *That's not like me. Tick. That is nothing like me. Tick. That isn't remotely like me. Tick.*

The resulting Least score represents your natural self. The Most like you element often takes a little more consideration. This represents how we feel we are seen by others or how we would like to be seen by others and merits a degree more thought – *Hmm, let me see now, yes that's me. Tick.*

WE ALL HAVE TO ADAPT TO SOME DEGREE

A simpler distinction between *Least* and *Most* is how we really are and how we behave outwardly i.e. at our place of work. The two graphs *Most* and *Least* will usually show a clear correlation but it is only reasonable that there will be differences. For example a natural High-I (buoyant) who worked as a mortician would be unlikely to produce a High-I *Most* graph. Or a natural Low-I who worked as a holiday camp Redcoat would expect to see a higher I score for her *persona*. We all have to adapt to our working environment. Where psychometric tests can be valuable is in identifying causes of stress. Clearly someone of an analytical High-C type who is cast in an extrovert High-I role will sooner or later find the personality conflict stressful. In the field of training, one can see natural High-Cs of very high intelligence, conscientious with great ability to absorb detailed information yet quite hopeless in front of a class, especially on longer courses. They have a total grasp of the course material but lack the people-skills for prolonged audience attention causing frustration for both trainer and class.

Conversely there are High-Is working in a High-C environment where they have had to suppress their natural ebullience and high-spirits. Over time they'll tell you they want to run out of the area screaming. Most common is the High-S salesperson working in a High-D sales environment where the culture is results-driven with an unrelenting demand for figures, performance, quotas, profit and almost no time for the more compassionate aspect of human interaction. A High-S in this situation will resent the constant, depersonalised grind for results and may well become stressed.

PSYCHOMETRICS AS A TOOL

The Introduction stressed that psychometric testing is a tool. As any tradesman knows, a quality tool used for its proper purpose will produce a quality finish. He also knows a screw can be driven home with a hammer and the job may appear adequately done.

One example of where psychometric preferences proved to be counterproductive was in a large sales-driven corporation. The personnel department carried out the preliminary interviews and forwarded a short list to the sales manager. Traditionally, personnel staff tend to be High-S (sympathetic, caring, people-oriented). Whichever the quadrant, we tend to prefer or recruit people from our own quadrant. It is human nature. Consequently, virtually all those on the short list of interviewees forwarded to the sales manager were from the S quadrant. The atmosphere amongst the sales force was most pleasant, with everyone ready to chat and enquire after one another. Alas, nobody was hitting target and the overall sales figures were a disaster.

This is not to say that High-Ss should not be in a hard selling environment. Not so, but there should be some tougher and more forceful cookies in there to set a standard and inject a degree of urgency and competitiveness into the sales effort.

DANGERS OF DO-IT-YOURSELF – WEIGHTING THE QUESTIONNAIRE

With any survey, it is not difficult to influence the answer by the way the question is worded. The political pollsters are well aware of this. 'Would you like to see the United Kingdom broken up?' and 'Would you like to see Scotland as an independent nation once again?' are in essence the same question. But one has a slightly negative overtone and the other a positive one. Similarly the pro-Europeans talk of the advantages of 'a single currency' whereas the Eurosceptics talk of 'abolishing the pound'. So with qualities in a psychometric test. 'Are you outgoing and friendly?' and 'Are you boisterous and loud?' – both typify the I type, but you might be more ready to identify with the former and reject the latter. The questionnaire (Fig 3) was compiled specially for this book and it does have a very slight built-in bias. Although accurate, should not be used for widespread analysis.

QUESTIONNAIRES PRODUCING FLAT GRAPHS

Many psychometric questionnaires are laid out in groups of four questions or statements. Each of the four represents the preferences of 4QB or in DISC terms, they reflect Dominance, Influencing, Supporting or Compliance.

A totally flat graph is found where you identify with an equal number of statements from each quadrant. It is seldom seen, but in any graph where the answers are all roughly equal, it is unwise to seek any firm deductive analysis. In the test, Fig 3, there are only twenty groups of statements so each answer contributes a five percent rise or fall in the graph. For example if you identified with the quadrants DISC with a score of 4, 5, 5, 6, then technically you could be classed as a Higher-C Lower-D, but with just a couple of different answers, you could be Higher-anything.

Flat graphs can be caused by several factors. One is where the person detects the pattern in the questions (not uncommon in the longer psychometric tests) and decides that having identified with, say, the D-Type quite a few times, she reflects that she might be considered too bossy or pushy, so she deliberately opts for statements or responses from other behaviour quadrants just for the sake of balance. This can produce a flat graph. In a recent case, a man with a flat graph turned out to have been unemployed for a year and not long divorced. Not unreasonably, his whole sense of self was distorted.

DOES YOUR 4QB PREFERENCE CHANGE ?

With your natural self, generally no. If you are born a High-C, that is almost certainly what you will remain. Some changes do occur with ageing. Younger High-D men tend to mellow with time – some do not. In manner, the dominance of the young Margaret Thatcher or Ian Paisley is indistinguishable from the old. High-I people can be affected by crises in life where self-confidence and self-esteem can be damaged. High-S people may attend Assertiveness Courses. They will probably remain High-S by nature but can learn how to take a stand and be more assertive. Even the detached High-C can be affected by exhortation such as the popular phrase, 'Get a life' and decide to party a bit more.

Your *Persona* or *Adapted Self* – the character you show in the workplace – may change from job to job. Someone who is by nature quite extrovert, loud and friendly may have to become more restrained, disciplined and assertive when given promotion with greater responsibilities.

HOW TO REMEMBER THE TYPES IN 4QB.

Picture a circle. You may well be able to commit to memory Jung's *Thinkers & Feelers* and their juxtaposition to his *Sensors & Intuitives*. These four points produce four clear quadrants giving the four specific types. Add Jung's divisions of *Introverts* to the left hemisphere and *Extroverts* to the right hemisphere and you have the base of psychological typology.

The best way to retain information is in pictures and it is easy to think geographically in terms of NORTH, SOUTH, EAST and WEST. The North conjures up images of Nordic coolness, thoughtfulness, undemonstrativeness and analytical types. The South is sunny, warm, tactile, family oriented and loving. That gives you the *Thinkers* and *Feelers*. For EAST and WEST, use the initials E & W to produce Expressive and Withdrawn. So if someone is in the NW corner of Jung's wheel you can identify a Withdrawn Northerner – the classic High-C type, Hippocrates' *Melancholic*. The compass point method has the advantage of being easily memorable and conflicts with no other recognised system.

Another variant is chosen by Insights International Ltd of Dundee who use colours to exemplify the four quadrants.

> **Dominant = Red**
> **Inspiring = Yellow**
> **Supporting = Green**
> **Calculating = Blue**

Yet another choice is to relate the quadrants to animals,

> **Dominant = Lion**
> **Inspiring = Porpoise**
> **Supportive = Labrador**
> **Calculating = Owl**

Adhering to the concept of *wholeness* for which the figure 4 is a universal symbol, some relate mankind's four primary preferences to the four elements – fire, air, earth and water. Fire being the assertive and dominant D; air representing the buoyant and inspiring I, earth is an obvious link with the nurturing and caring S and water symbolising the cool and reflective C. The choice is yours but if you wish to pursue your interest in psychometrics, the international DISC is the most commonly used.

CASE STUDIES

The 'Plastic D'

Martin's background was financial service sales. The style had been consultative, calm, conversational and unaggressive. This matched his personality (High-S) and he had been successful in that field. He moved to another industry in the role of sales manager where the company culture was High-D. The sales director's addresses to the sales force were bombastic, dictatorial and aggressive, inviting no comment or feedback. Any sales manager not practising this style was considered, weak, ineffectual and a wimp. Consequently Martin adopted this dominant persona at his sales meetings but increasingly he found it went against the grain and his apprehension grew with each meeting. Martin found himself growing tenser and more stressed. His stays in the pub after work grew longer and, though never absent in his previous job, he found himself taking the odd day off. As a result, fewer sales meetings took place or they were delegated to the team leaders. After a series of training courses run for the sales staff which included the principles of psychometrics, Martin acquired the nick-name, 'The Plastic D'.

The Owl and the Pussycat

Still with the same organisation, the managing director was a classic Owl, a High-C whose background was accountancy. He was highly intelligent and a great long term strategist. However his preference was for sets of figures, computer printouts and fiscal analysis. He was also quite shy when it came to human interaction. His sales director as we have seen above was a total lion (a big cat as opposed to a pussycat, forgive the licence). He was more abrasive than assertive, impatient, autocratic and utterly dominant. During a quite long absence of the sales director, the MD had to take over his role. He did not attempt to adopt the High-D style but delivered his addresses in his own High-C style with detailed analysis of performance in graphs, pie-charts and sets of figures. The salespeople's heads went down as they were mainly High-I and were either confused or bored to distraction. One absolute must for salespeople is stimulation and motivation.

QUESTIONS

Q. *I'm a successful salesperson and a natural Supporter or Amiable, I'm being made a Team Leader. Should I adapt my style to Dominant?*

A. Although we all have to adapt to the working environment, attempts at profound change will create stress which, over time, can manifest itself in all sorts of problems such as loss of confidence, nervous habits, higher alcohol intake, smoking or absenteeism. If you are a natural High-S, you should try to run your team on your strengths i.e harmony, cooperation, teamwork and trust. The hairy-chested macho style is common in sales, but that is your diametric opposite or 'blind spot' and adapting to it will not only cause you stress but will appear unnatural to others.

Q. *Would an Assertiveness Course help?*

A. An Assertiveness Course should ideally teach you how to maximise your personality and use your strengths to their greatest effect. It should help you develop a revised style of delivery rather than attempt to change your natural psychological disposition.

Q. *My problem is that I'm too assertive – what can I do?*

A. Precisely the same principle applies, rather like the converse of an Assertiveness Course. Take Margaret Thatcher – her image was seen as too dominant and abrasive, so the spin-doctors tried to soften her image both visually and aurally. Her voice became deeper and her speech slower. She was still the same Iron Lady but the edges received a good sandpapering. With such a forceful woman, the changes were less perceptible than with someone else but she was returned for a third term.

4

Applications –

At Work and At Play

RECRUITING

Before looking at what psychometric analysis can do, it is prudent to establish what it cannot do. It cannot gauge qualities such as intelligence, ability or morality. Skilled recruiters will ascertain qualifications, levels of experience, success in previous roles and character references before even thinking in psychometric terms. Some companies reverse the process, with applicants first being asked to complete a lengthy personality test of around 200 questions, taking up to an hour. This is then followed by an interview of perhaps no more than twenty minutes. The applicant is given the bad impression that an impersonal questionnaire is more important that a face-to-face interview.

I.Q.

Let us look at intelligence. Prisons are full of High-D men with low IQs. Their natural tendency is to assert. Their weakness is aggression (see page 51). If you are highly intelligent and articulate, the need to shift from assertion to aggression is assuaged by the gift of lucid argument and persuasive rhetoric. With limited intelligence the High-D can spiral from the need for assertion, to frustration, to aggression to violence. The maxim, *Violence is the product of an exhausted mind,* is particularly apposite in the case of a mind which is easily exhausted.

It is not difficult to spot the High-I with a low IQ. He is quite harmless. He is the one for whom canned laughter was invented. He'll stand at the bar, eyes transfixed by the TV, laughing at some vacuous game show or manufactured comedy, maybe even missing some of the comedy lines but enjoying himself nonetheless. The IQ of the High-S and High-C are less noticeable being on the introvert side of the circle (West side for Withdrawn) so they can be in a world of their own, to use that human if non-scientific phrase.

ACCENTUATE THE POSITIVE BUT DON'T FORGET THE NEGATIVE

When psychometric analysis is used in recruiting there may be a tendency to concentrate on the strengths of a type and over-look the weaknesses. Take the High-I for example. Buoyant, ebullient, friendly, creative and spontaneous – just the person we need for a tour guide or cabin crew on an airline or selling some upbeat goods or service. Or perhaps a team leader or even a sales trainer. But remember the downside – interrupting, irritating, too keen to be liked, fickle and lacking depth.

Personnel staff are often High-S (SW quadrant) and frequently recruit their own clones. This is no bad thing as they are genuinely concerned about people and relationships. They accept that staff can have compassionate problems and may go sick, whereas the more hairy-chested High-D manager is intolerant of such weaknesses and dismisses them accordingly. However the High-S can be maddeningly counterproductive at times. For example, when an employee is clearly underperforming in every aspect of the job and is disruptive, noncooperative and absent on a regular basis, the more assertive manager knows that the point of no return has come and dismissal is the only option. The High-S personnel person will lose focus and get bogged down in procedure. How many verbal warnings were given? Dates? What interval specified for improvement? How many written warnings given? Dates? Intervals for improvement? Were the warnings witnessed? Is there evidence of the verbal warnings? Are there copies of the written warnings? Were they on company note paper? Were copies sent to Personnel? We know procedures are necessary but when somebody is literally more trouble than he is worth, they simply have to go (bearing in mind the provisions of employment law!).

Negativity can be born of compassion

Out of the workplace, the High-S can lack focus and be negative. You give the High-S some little personal detail (they like that)...

'We're off on holiday next month', you offer.
'Oh lovely, where are you off to?'
'We thought of Majorca'
'Won't it be too hot at this time of year? It's not the cheapest time of year either. Have you thought about the school holiday? The airports will be packed and all the popular resorts will be very busy this time of year. You be careful about that Legionnaires Disease or was it an outbreak of E-Coli I read about'

By the time the High-S is finished, you won't want to go. Yes, don't tell me, you know somebody's mother who is just like that. It is not that the High-S is being negative to spoil your plan or enjoyment – quite the reverse. It is because the High-S is caring, considerate and into human relationships that they express these concerns. If the person is a mother as well, with all the normal maternal instincts, the overprotectiveness can be profound.

Recruit the High-S for the strengths of that quadrant but be conscious of the weaknesses.

The High-C is invaluable. They make excellent engineers, scientists, financial directors, accountants, and librarians . They will undertake painstaking research, they can work without being subject to distraction. Not only will they take on a task requiring lengthy and deep concentration, more importantly the result will almost certainly be accurate. But remember, that is their gift, so don't crowd them, don't hurry them, don't expect them to drop everything and hurry along to old Fred's farewell presentation and don't drag them up to sing a Karaoke number at the staff party. That is not their way. Leave all that to the I's and to a lesser extent the D's and S's.

Tim Luckhurst, the Assistant Editor of *The Scotsman*, gives a description of Kevin Marsh, a senior executive with BBC news and current affairs. He writes (12 August 97):

He is incisive, adept at lateral thinking and very loud. He behaves like a B-Movie stereotype of a newspaper editor. He wears red braces. He shouts, swears and upsets staff and contributors alike. He does not suffer fools at all, let alone gladly. One senior Radio 4 editor who once worked for Marsh at The World at One said yesterday, 'He is a very aggressive man. I was terrified of him. By the end of the programme I'd be emotionally exhausted and I'd go into the lavatory for a rest. Kevin once burst in on me in order to pursue his point'

Despite his overbearing and sometimes bullying manner and his intellectual arrogance, Marsh is highly regarded by his staff. He has insulted many of them at least once and nobody would call him cuddly but Kevin is clever and loyal. Above all he is principled...

Luckhurst goes on some more but the extract above is quite enough. The detail is so perfectly descriptive of a High-D that it could almost be lifted word for word from any good textbook on psychometric types.

THE CAP MAY NOT ALWAYS FIT

There are dangers in taking an over-simplistic view of psycho-metric testing with regard to recruitment. Using the 4QB description *DEAA – Driver, Expressive, Amiable, Analytical* it could be reasoned that managers should be selected from the Drivers; salespeople from the Expressives; nurses, social workers and other carers from the Amiables and accountants, scientists and technicians from the Analyticals. Certainly some famous leaders were Drivers/Assertives. Margaret Thatcher is a perfect example but her downside of abrasiveness and unyieldingness caused her party to rally against her and depose her. John Major's gift was his amiableness which made him personally very popular, particularly when viewed alongside his predecessor. But it was Major's very amiableness which allowed him to be surrounded by some of the least attractive politicians Westminster had ever seen and they in turn contributed to one of the greatest electoral defeats this century.

NATIONAL PREFERENCES

The culture of companies or nations can vary dramatically. The High-D Thatcher at the height of her popularity could have matched any PM in history, even that other Dominant, Churchill. The French, though expressive, prefer their leaders as Cs – Mitterand and D'Estaing being just two rather dour and detached examples. The Americans on the other hand go for the High-Is such as Clinton and Reagan. They tried a High-C, Nixon, but regretted it. The South Americans have a history of choosing High-Ds. Perhaps it is their respect for rhetoric and passion but alas their preference has inflicted upon them more despots than any other corner of the planet. It can be a vicious circle because it takes a High-D to depose a dictator so the same type is back in charge, for good or ill.

Company culture

The cultures of various organisations also vary. Hospitals and social work groups tend to exude a High-S aura while many sales driven companies are very High-D. If you fly Easijet, you'll find the entire staff seem to be High-I. Some high-tech organisations radiate a quiet and academic High-C atmosphere from the reception area to right throughout the building.

One unfortunate side-effect of strong cultures is where staff try too hard to adapt. Many sales driven companies with a High-D culture have Sales Managers who tend to resemble *The Scotsman* description of the BBC executive. Alas some Field Sales Managers or Team Leaders from other quadrants try desperately to emulate this hairy-chested style and at best come across as phoney or "plastic Ds" – at worst they put themselves under stress which can be debilitating.

JOHN ADAIR'S THREE CIRCLES – TEAM, TASK & INDIVIDUAL

DOUGLAS MCGREGOR – 'X' & 'Y' THEORY

The post-war years produced a number of industrial psychologists and management gurus. A.H. Maslow has already been mentioned. Two contemporaries of his were John Adair and Douglas McGregor. We tend to remember the current gurus such as John Harvey Jones, Tom Peters, and Charles Handy but Adair, McGregor and Maslow were the stars of the 1940s and 50s. Adair argued that any corporate or organisational dynamic had three component parts, the TEAM, the TASK and the INDIVIDUAL. He likened them to three interactive and overlapping circles, each having an influence on the others, but never overwhelming them. All could be expressed as needs which had to be met for the organisation or group to succeed – each individual involved had specific personal, professional and social needs to be met; the task had to be clear and completed; the team had to operate as an efficient, co-ordinated body. Imbalances cause distress and failure.

Each circle is of equal importance. The three are interconnected and they should exist in harmony keeping the organisation running smoothly. If any one ceases to function properly or becomes detached the organisation comes to a halt. Though generally thought of in a business context, Adair's principles apply to any collective, a military unit, a football team or a group of friends on a touring holiday.

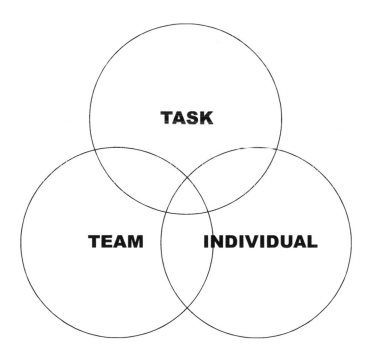

Fig. 8

THE 'INDIVIDUAL' ELEMENT AT FAULT

For example, the working unit might be the family. The Task is to have an enjoyable holiday. The Team is Mum, Dad and two kids and the Individuals are all four with their personal preferences, wants and needs. This should be simple enough, but Dad (a D) decides they'll all go to the west of Ireland so he can enjoy peace and quiet and do some fishing. Mum wanted more sophistication and to get some sun while the kids wanted excitement. So, by one Individual selfishly asserting his wishes, the Team is divided and the Task is not accomplished.

Similarly, too much favouritism shown to an Individual in a family, a working team, a school class or a sports team can alienate the Team and jeopardise the Task.

'TEAM' ELEMENT AT FAULT

On a Team Building weekend, the team concerned were not given the details until a few days before. The team of eight included two ex-army men, one man from Northern Ireland and two women. The enthusiastic organiser, a management trainer from Surrey, had arranged a 'Paint-Ball, Secret Mission' weekend. For the unfamiliar, this is a war game where team members are issued with rifles which fire balls of paint at the 'enemy'. A mission is designed and players crawl through a wood or moorland to achieve their goal exchanging rifle fire en route. The management trainer had run a similar exercise for some trainee accountants from the Home Counties and it had been a wow. Not so with this bunch. The two ex-soldiers considered the idea quite infantile. The man from Northern Ireland found it difficult to enthuse about being a sniper and the two females didn't fancy crawling on their stomachs through damp bracken and fern. The remaining three were quite keen and argued with the others.

In this true example, the emphasis was laid on the the Team.

The objective was well-intentioned – bind them together in different circumstances outside the work place. However, no-one considered the Individual. So the Individuals were hostile, the Team dissolved and the Task was not accomplished.

How would you have approached it? Of course, you would have approached the team earlier and asked them what they would like to do. Even if the idea is not particularly brilliant, as long as the participants feel part of the decision making process they are more likely to support that decision.

'TASK' AT FAULT

Many large corporations are Task driven, with a High-D culture. They are quoted on the stock market. The board is answerable to the shareholders. The executives are answerable to the board. The executives bawl at the heads of departments, the managers threaten their staff. Service engineers are given too many tasks per day. Salespeople have to produce their 'key ratio sheets' – how many doors did you knock? How many contacts did you make? How many presentations made? How many closes did you make? How many orders? How many appointed call-backs made? Numbers, results, successes, failures, threats and worse – when the salespeople do produce consistently good figures, the goalposts tend to get moved and new targets are set, perpetuating the treadmill grind.

Let's make it clear, the concept of a Task driven company is sound. Everyone in business must have daily, weekly and monthly targets, clear profit margins and key ratios. The danger is where the Task becomes all-important to a degree where the Team and the Individual become so subordinate as to be crushed in the process. The Task is to run a profitable and successful business, but when the teams and individuals feel undervalued, unappreciated and demoralised, the synergy factor suffers and the teams drift apart. This results in high staff turnover, constant recruiting and training and the associated massive expenditure of both time and money. Because of the constant need for staff, corners can get cut and decisions made in haste, resulting in lower standards and continuation of the problem. So, though a High-D culture is good, it should be balanced with an appreciation of 4QB and some applied Maslow.

Canon, the office equipment multinational, had a good sense of balance. Yes, the salespeople were Task driven but their OTE (on target earnings) were fair, their company cars were of a good standard, expenses were reasonable and sales incentives were always quality ones – holidays in the West Indies, Indian Ocean, the USA, or sometimes on a cruise liner. Recognition took many forms, not least being on stage at some prestige venue to receive an achievement award. Salesmen were given grades and cars commensurate with the grade. The stick can be bearable providing there are ample carrots. The company that is Task obsessed to the detriment of the other two circles deserves the organisational machinery to run out of kilter or stop entirely.

Understanding John Adair's three circles of equal importance is essential when viewing psychometric types in a corporate environment. Task driven organisations tend to recruit and attract the High-D type. Unfortunately High-D types seldom go on courses so they've never heard of John Adair and even if they did, they would probably consider all that talk about Teams and Individuals as being for wimps. So, ironically, when a High-D, hairy-chested manager is recruited by a Task driven company, they see him as part of the solution towards Task accomplishment, but alas, he is also part of the problem.

MCGREGOR'S THEORY X AND THEORY Y

McGregor defined two styles of management:

The X Theory. This was the traditional style of management (though it is not dead yet) where the management has a set of objectives and it controls the staff, organising, instructing, and monitoring workrate, productivity, time-keeping, use of materials and equipment – in essence, an authoritarian regime. Bluntly the workers are really not to be trusted. Unsupervised they will be indolent or even disruptive because they do not understand management policies or practices nor do they care.

The Y Theory. This is the opposite of X. The workers can be trusted. Get rid of the indignities such as clocking-on. People take a natural pride in a job well done and are motivated by achievement and enjoy exercising their initiative. Management agrees given objectives with the staff and the workers are left to accomplish those objectives. In being given respect and responsibility for the task, the worker is more likely to take ownership of the task and see it through efficiently.

McGregor was very much in tune with Maslow and argued the hierarchy of needs strongly and simply. He distinguished the lower needs from the higher by calling them physiological needs and psychological needs i.e the physical ones being food, drink, warmth, comfort, protection. The psychological ones being status, recognition and importance. The traditional manager would complain about the workers thus, *'What's the matter with these damn people? I pay them good money but they just don't give me their best'*.

Maslow and McGregor identified that man lives not by bread alone and if the boss was more aware of dignity, recognition, pride and those higher factors in the hierarchy he could expect greater loyalty and a more productive performance.

As we welcome the 21st century, the Y Theory may seem just plain common sense. But the second world war was a cathartic time for industrial relations. Virtually the entire male population of Britain had been imbued with military management styles – very much the X method of obedience – do it now, chop chop – you're not paid to think, laddie. The rigid class system was breaking down. Full employment prevailed. Trade unions grew strong. A welfare state had been introduced. Men were no longer terrified of losing a job with the concomitant risks of near starvation and eviction. Once subservient women who only got the vote in 1918 (if over 30 – reduced to age 21 in 1928) were becoming more confident after their invaluable work during the war.

Bearing in mind that McGregor wrote his book, *The Human Side of Enterprise* in 1957, he was quite advanced. However he did come from America where the iniquities of the British class system were unknown. In one chapter of his book he alludes to U.S. companies who experimented with 'self-appraisal' systems. Imagine that in the UK! Here we are used to the manager painstakingly going through performance, factor after factor, with some hapless employee.

To some extent, the two descriptions – the X manager and the Y manager – are caricatures at either end of a continuous scale. Absolute X and absolute Y are rare, with most managers or organisations adopting a position somewhere along the scale, but with an orientation towards one end or the other.

Where an Adair TASK-driven company existed with a McGregor X-style management you had the classic *sweat shop* or some dark, satanic mill. Though McGregor did not use applied psychometrics per se in essence his X and Y management styles were wholly compatible with High-D and High-S respectively.

TEAM BUILDING – FOCUSED TEAMS OR BALANCED TEAMS?

An example of a focused team was at the Iranian embassy siege where the SAS abseiled from the roof and took the building in a lightning strike of split second precision. Although the SAS will have all four quadrants in the regiment, this was a High-D operation. No High-S anxiety, *'Be careful now, Corporal'* or High-

I frivolities, *'Last one down is a fairy'*, nor any High-C *'Can we just go over the plans once more'*. This was strictly a *'Right, let's do it!'* operation.

Focused teams are invaluable in certain circumstances but the more common is the balanced team. Most sales teams should be balanced teams with representation from each quadrant, the proportion depending on the goods or services being sold. Airline cabin crew for example would be predominantly I and S – both friendly and caring. However C would be useful to ensure all safety procedures were followed and all the logistic requirements were correct.

Similarly with any expedition. A team setting out to climb Mount Everest should be well balanced. The D would be impatient to get going. The I would be inspirational, encouraging and cheery while the S would notice that someone wasn't looking well or had developed a limp or other personal problem. The C would be the only one to have studied the weather report in detail or noticed that there was a shortfall in tent pegs, tins of beans, oxygen, water or toilet rolls.

The D would be getting impatient, nagging everyone, *'Come on, let's go!'* This type is usually the hero in all the movies.

It is quite unfair really – the eastern hemisphere (Expressives and Extroverts), the John Waynes and Gene Kellys, get all the glory while the western hemisphere (Withdrawn) save lives.

A High-D delegate on a course had to be put down when he said that the Ds get things done and it is they who win the wars. It was pointed out to him that they were also more likely to start them.

BALANCED TEAMS – THAT'S SHOWBUSINESS

The symbol of wholeness has always been the circle. It has also been represented by the figure four. We often refer to the four corners of the earth or four-square. So it is quite consistent that

Hippocrates should have quantified man's Four Humours or that Jung should have used a circle in developing the Jungian Wheel to encompass man's diversity.

We know instinctively that there are different types and we read the psychometric descriptions with little surprise as they only confirm what we inwardly knew.

Good dramatists have always written their plays on the balanced team principle. Four centuries before Jung, Shakespeare knew full well the importance of distinct characterisation. Perhaps the most common balance in plays, movies or books is the High-D hero and the High-S leading lady. He took on the world at fencing, in a shoot out, a fist fight, a chariot race or some insuperable challenge while she was always ready to bathe the wounds, mop his brow or cradle his noble head. It just wouldn't work if he rode home to a High-D Margaret Thatcher type (however glamorous):

'Where have you been? Look at the state of you. What time do you call this? A flask of wine and a warm embrace is it? Get your own bloody wine, I'm off to my Townswomen's Guild Assertiveness Course.'

Frequently the character balance is in the two main characters. The ever popular *Dad's Army* has the D-type Capt Mainwaring who is abrupt, assertive and impatient. He is balanced beautifully by Sgt Wilson who is wholly S – kind, caring, gentle and slow to any form of anger or condemnation. Granted the portrayals have to be good and the script must sparkle but it is the characterisation we relish.

THE GOLDEN GIRLS

Occasionally all four quadrants are included. Then, with good acting and a good script you have a successful show. On first viewing *The Golden Girls*, one knew it was good but couldn't quite understand why. It was about four women. There was little or no action. It was shot entirely in the studio and the strength of the show seemed to be the interaction between the four main characters. Channel hopping on cable, one was further surprised to see the show on several foreign channels. With dubbing and translation, surely the dialogue would have to suffer and as the show was dependent on the verbal exchanges, how could it sustain international appeal? The only deduction was that the characters were so strong. With a deeper grasp of 4QB one can recognise the four quadrants so clearly and it becomes easier to understand why *The Golden Girls* appeals so much. Whether psychometricians or not we recognise the wholeness of the characterisation.

Dorothy, the tall one with the deep voice is the D. She is the boss about the house. Blanche, the Southern belle who just loves to party is the typical I. Rose, the ultra-caring bleeding heart has S stamped all the way through and the wee, calculating, undemonstrative, tough cookie of a mother completes the circle with her C portrayal.

RISING DAMP

Once you begin to identify these types in a stage or screen context, examples tend to spring to mind. The British example which portrays all four types in an excellent balance was *Rising Damp*. The bossy landlord, Rigsby, filled the D quadrant. His diametric opposite was the compassionate Miss Jones. The I quadrant was filled by the Richard Beckensale character. He played the young medical student who loved fun and was preoccupied with having a good time. His diametric opposite was the exquisite African noble, Philip, who was cool, serious and detached. Of course the script and acting sparkled but it was the sense of wholeness which made the show such a success.

Where dramatists can go wrong is when they need a certain course of action to take place and for convenience or expediency they make, for example, a C character carry out a typically I action or a D act like a S. Or they simply want to alter the tempo or mood of the drama but choose the wrong type to change it. We all know and use the phrase *acting out of character*. We cannot define it precisely but we know it when we see it.

One example was the James Bond movie where George Lazenby played the ultra tough 007. Bond's girlfriend is killed at one stage in the high action drama. Next we see Bond in floods of tears. Quite human really but not for the lady in the stalls who hissed scornfully, 'James Bond in tears, well really!'

TEAM BUILDING – SPORT

The British Lions 1997 rugby team set a precedent by calling in the assistance of management consultants. The problem was simple enough, it was teamwork. The Lions squad is made up of the cream of the home teams, England, Scotland, Wales and Ireland. Throughout the winter season these home nations compete with each other and with France for the Championship title, the Triple Crown (British Isles only) and the Calcutta Cup (Scotland and England only). The rivalry is fierce and the passion is high. Big strong men can shed a tear.

When the last song has faded, the stands are silent and the groundsmen are busy replacing the divots on the battlefields, the best of these men come together to form the Lions and go on tour. They tour the southern hemisphere to play great rugby nations such as New Zealand, Australia or South Africa.

These men who until recently had fought each other to exhaustion and maybe had their hearts broken (along with the odd bone) now have to bind together to form a dynamic team to take on the best in the world. Not being privy to the management consultants' brief, one cannot be too precise, but the fact they were called in at all is a clear indication of what was required. These Celts and Anglo Saxons had to be made to gell together and function as a unit. The steps are very straightforward:

1. **Self-respect**
2. **Individual respect**
3. **Mutual respect**
4. **Team respect**

First imbue the man with self-respect. Remove any doubts about his own personal ability, skill, attitude and superiority. Next encourage him to have the same belief in the other individuals, to value and respect the others' qualities and, most importantly, the differences. A simple example might be that a lean winger with lightning acceleration must respect and value the power of a mighty forward who is less fleet of foot. From this follows mutual respect which in turn broadens into total team respect. The fact that a man is English, Irish, Welsh or a Scot becomes irrelevant (though you can guarantee, never forgotten). Whatever the methods of the management consultants, the '97 Lions team had the most successful tour of South Africa anyone can remember. The South African Springboks are seldom beaten on their own territory and never intimidated. A Pretorian one-liner is:

What's the definition of a gay in Pretoria? A man who prefers women to rugby!

The last truly great Lions squad was led by the Irish captain Willie John McBride. It was no coincidence that Willie John himself was a man of great stature, a fine player, courteous and a gentleman.

His natural authority, warmth and sheer decency were enough to command the affection and respect of the team and thereby diminish any national or personal differences.

Attitude is everything. It was the *laager mentality* of the South African which forged together the fierce determination to win and show the world. New Zealand's All Blacks are rugby legends and sweep all opposition before them, yet they come from a nation of only three million people. Wales, with a similar population, in its heyday consistently won on passion. When their performance deteriorated, so alas, did their morale, producing a self-perpetuating spiral for too many years. Scotland manages to produce its fiercest performance against The Auld Enemy, England.

Most of the great football managers had probably never heard of John Adair but they instinctively knew how to operate the three circles of TASK, TEAM & INDIVIDUAL in perfect harmony. Stein, Busby, Shankley and Alex Ferguson all come from that hard West of Scotland school where real men don't smile and to smile on the Sabbath was to be in league with the devil. Their granite faces would have the unknowing believe they were all TASK obsessed managers. When he permitted himself the odd expression of happiness, Stein's dour expression, conditioned by the Lanarkshire pits, would be transformed by a smile so radiant it lit up his entire face. The warmth and compassion of the man became all apparent and, though a TASK-master, you knew that his warmth had to affect his players.

Observers who are not familiar with the Lanarkshire breed can believe that the dourness is deep rooted but you have to know the type to understand the keen humour of such men. Shankley's reply to the the comment that he seemed to view football as a matter of life and death is often quoted. Shankley answered, *'It's much more important than that.'* Many took this at face value, not appreciating the deadpan delivery of West of Scotland wit.

Jack Charlton had the same gift for man management with the Irish team. When Ireland reached the quarter finals of the World Cup in Italy, the tension on the players must have been immense but Jack walked amongst the players ruffling their hair and telling the lads they had done brilliantly in getting that far and they should relax and go and enjoy the game of football. Other managers might have hectored the players not to let their country down or some other pressure-building exhortation.

Jack Charlton's task with the Irish football team had strong similarities with the uniting of the Lions rugby squad. There were virtually no suitable players playing in Ireland's own league. All the Irish talent was playing for the major English, Scottish or Continental clubs. The FAI (Football Association of Ireland) became tagged as Find An Irishman and the FIFA ruling of allowing grandsons of ethnic nationals to represent the country of origin produced a most extraordinary mix of football talent. The players sang the Irish National Anthem in Cockney and other English accents. The blood line was Irish, English, Scottish, West Indian, Italian and who knows where else but the strength of unity in the team was both impressive and moving.

Big Jack had all the key ingredients. First he had respect. He, with his brother Bobby, had been part of the 1966 World Cup winning English squad. He'd seen it, done it and got the innumerable shirts. Jack could also have come from the same Lanarkshire mould as Stein and Busby. He was big, tough, straight, blunt and very much a man's man. He liked a pint and the solitude of fishing. Though English, Jack's commitment to his team was total. Snipers have commented that being turned down for the England manager's job may have strengthened his resolve for Ireland. This is unfair. No man of integrity takes on a task of such magnitude unless he is prepared to give it his absolute best. It was because of Charlton's devotion to his team and task that the loyalty and respect which the individuals returned to him was so great.

Dr George Sik of the management consultants and psychometric specialists Saville and Holdsworth has written a book specifically on football management called *I Think I'll Manage*. The book is co-authored by Pat Nevin, the Scottish internationalist. Sik says that the most successful managers and coaches are the ones who treated players as individuals needing different approaches to bring out the best in them.

Regarding Adair, Newton or Maslow's Hierarchy, the point was made earlier that whenever some philosophy is expounded clearly and simply we may tend to think to ourselves, *that's obvious!* But it only becomes obvious when considerable research has gone into formulating the theory and then expressing it in its simplest form. So with George Sik, and even the *that's obvious* type is still capable of understanding the message but forgetting to apply it.

Too many managers, football or otherwise, shout and bawl at their troops, insisting on results and tongue-lashing them when they fail. This is bad management, especially regarding failure. When a team loses or a salesman blanks or a tender for business is lost, in most cases the failure in itself is more than enough reproof for the individual(s) concerned. Look at a losing team's heads hung down. The verbal battering from a manager is often quite unnecessary. With a commission-only sales force which was required to produce a fixed number of orders, the look on the salesperson's face conveyed the failure. By the manager asking if there was any point in saying anything he achieved all he needed. The answer was always, *'No. I feel bad enough. I'm gutted. But it won't happen again.'* A reply of, *'Good lad, now get back out there and sell,'* was as effective as any verbal onslaught.

QUESTIONS

Q. How does understanding 4QB help in working with people?

A. Take the tyrant sales director where many went in fear of his outbursts. The problem with High-Ds is that, because of their drive, they often occupy management positions. Few people appreciate psychometric typology, so when the High-D has a fiery staff meeting (à la Mr Kevin Marsh) and leaves everyone just about trembling, our High-D manager goes away and completely forgets about his ranting. There is nothing personal whatever in his blasts. He is results driven and his personality dictates that the best way to achieve results is to demand them forcefully. So when he cheerfully greets one of his staff half an hour later, the staff member is still smarting with hurt and maybe thinking dark thoughts whereas the manager is oblivious to such sensitivities. By understanding the type it takes the sting out of apparently personal attacks.

Q. Do high-tech companies, for example, recruit High-C staff ?

A. Not necessarily, While doing consultancy work with an Information Technology company, I was surprised during the initial discussions to find how well the Sales Director got on with the Personnel Manager. Frequently these are D and S respectively and are blind spots for each other, producing a strained relationship. They obliged me with a psychometric test each and I was pleased to note they were both High-I, working well and socialising together. Further investigation revealed that the American parent company valued psychometrics and chose to encourage a High-I culture because the whole aura of Information Technology was High-C. They reckoned that too many High-Cs in a High-C industry could have a stultifying effect on the people working in the field.

Q. *Surely a football team of eleven of the best players in the world would beat any team, irrespective of quadrants ?*

A. If the team was formed to play a one-off exhibition match the answer is probably yes. However, in the real sense of teamwork, teams have to train together, take planes, buses and trains together, eat together and share hotels sometimes over long periods. So though the balance of skills is important, the balance of personality, respect and motivation will determine the long term success of a team. Brian Clough in his heyday took Nottingham Forest from the fourth division to the first with virtually no changes to the team.

5

Perception

"O wad some Pow'r the giftie gie us
To see oursels as others see us"

Robert Burns knew that any form of posturing or artificiality was worthless. He completes this stanza with

"It wad frae mony a blunder free us
and foolish notion"

Perhaps it's because we do not fully understand ourselves that we try to emulate qualities we admire or envy in others. In Dr Jolande Jacobi's book, *The Psychology of C G Jung*, she writes on The Realisation of Self '...it leads the individual to know himself for what he naturally is, as distinguished from what he would like to be and probably nothing is more difficult for a human being.'

Of course there are many confusions in life. Homosexual men brought up by a macho father have a whole set of identity problems. Although attracted by the same sex, at least they enjoy being male. What of the unfortunate transsexual totally convinced of a perceived sexuality but trapped in the body of the opposite gender.

We tend to snigger at the balding, overweight and ageing man who struggles to get out of a low, sleek sports car. Our vocabulary is full of anti-*foolish notion* terms such as, *Grow up;*

Act your age; Just be yourself; Who do you think you are; Mutton dressed as lamb; Phoney; Plastic and Pretentious to choose only a few.

But leave all those confusions and artificialities to one side. Let's stick to the basic four quadrants. In business, if the company culture is High-D, many line managers try to emulate this style when it is not inherently theirs. This rests uncomfortably on both the line manager and the staff who report to him. If you accept the quadrant to which you belong and recognise all its merits and demerits you are well along the road to self realisation.

Example

You are a line manager who is naturally High-S and you prefer to lead in your own specific style. Rather than demand autocratically, you will prefer to use harmony and cooperation. With new systems or disciplines, you will consult with your team, discuss, handle questions and objections and reach agreement. Okay, if you cannot reach agreement you may have to assert authority (if unable, you shouldn't be in a management position in the first place). But your preference is harmony. Conflicts may arise, a superior line manager (a High-D) may condemn your S style with, *'Don't be so bloody soft with them. You just tell them. If they don't like it just tell them to give you their car keys and bugger off.'*

Here you have two options: stay as you are or become a Plastic D with chest wig and a more macho style. This is doomed to failure for two reasons:

i) The line manager you wish to impress is a High-D who is generally oblivious to personalities and subtleties of style. Just as you think you are succeeding in your *adapted style (persona)* your boss will come and attack you from an entirely different angle.

ii) You put unnecessary stress upon yourself and persistent acting out of character will lead eventually to problems of either a psychological or physiological nature, such as loss of confidence, anxiety, headaches, feeling run down or self indulgence of some kind, probably alcohol.

The armed forces know something of man-management. One axiom gained from twelve years' naval service is, *The ideal situation is to gain respect and affection but if you have to lose one, keep the respect.* Very sound. In the above example you are more likely to command both by being genuine. By opting for the Plastic D role you will probably lose both. Shakespeare put it with great wisdom and succinctness in Hamlet:

'*This above all; to thine own self be true. And it must follow, as the night the day, Thou canst not then be false to any man.*'

CASE STUDY

At the end-of-year bash for a large office equipment dealership, the MD's speech was the main event before we all got heavily into the free bar. The MD was a High-C with an accountancy background, a good chief executive, quite popular and quite well respected. His Regional Sales Manager was a naturally gifted speaker with that superb knack of delivering a rising crescendo which was inspirational and motivational. He was about 50/50 D/I which in Jungian terms is the Intuitive Extrovert or using the terms of other psychometric companies a *Shaper; Motivator; Expressive Driver; Explorer or Promoter.* Alas the MD was none of these things but he felt he had to compete with his RSM. He must have worked hard in his preparation. The theme of his speech, naturally enough, was how the company had fared in the dying year, with some figures, some good achievements, some personal mentions and a round of applause where merited. Then he could move up a gear and exhort the troops to even greater things in the coming year while painting a rosy picture of successes for staff and company alike.

The script was not bad but his attempts at rising inflection with accompanying arm raising and the clenching of a fist were so unnatural as to render the delivery embarrassing. At the high points when he should have been eyeball to eyeball with his audience, he tended to look at his script thus losing the entire conviction and any spontaneity of delivery.

To thine own self be true

Although the Bards of Scotland and England both cautioned against artificiality, there is little doubt that we shall continue to make the same mistakes and adapt ourselves to conform to prevailing pressure.

Self realisation is not just healthy for the psyche, it is the only way to a non-stressed *modus vivendi*. You will always have some level of stress, so do not burden yourself with unnecessary amounts. Any so-called self-improvement course should begin by recognising your gifts and preferences.

An Assertiveness course, for example, should not try to change a High-S into a High-D, it should teach how to assert a position or argument through the strengths of an S.

Take the example where the D-type boss tells his line manager not to be so soft. Remember, softness is the boss's perception and is a totally subjective term. His perception is disapproving and he condemns it as being weak. Mistake No 1 is to believe his perception is the correct one. Mistake No 2 would be to attempt to conform to his concept of tough man-management.

The way to be assertive in response to this pressure would be to be completely honest, such as, *'Look boss, your objectives and mine are exactly the same. You are right about the figures but the way you manage and the way I manage are different. You have a gift for authority, mine is more for cooperation. It may not work for you* but it works for me. I can't copy you. My team would see through it immediately. I'd come across as a phoney. So I'll work at getting the figures up but I'm going to have to do it my way."

There is nothing aggressive in the assertion. It is honest, reasonable and factual. But most of all, it is not being overcompliant or role playing. It is, to use the modern IT phrase, WYSIWYG (pronounced Wissy-wig) – What You See Is What You Get. The boss may disagree and may not like your view but High-Ds tend to be fair and principled and although he may respond with some choice four-letter words, you'll gain more respect than an attempt at conformity.

YOUR PERCEPTION IS YOUR REALITY.

One of the Perception Exercises used on courses is where the OHP screen displays the drawing of two-faces-in-one (Fig 9 – see overleaf).

This one is the picture which contains both the face of an old crone and a pretty young girl. Delegates are asked to write on a piece of paper two things – one, the age of the female they see and two, a single descriptive term.

The group is usually split roughly 50/50. Half write down something like, 25, Pretty; 22, Elegant; or 24, Attractive. The other half comment, 75, Ugly; 70, A witch; or 80, A hag.

When asking the group to read out what they have written those who see the young girl look up in shock when they hear the 'old hag' comments. Those who see the old woman look unbelievingly at those who claim they see a bonny 20 year old.

This exercise is valuable from two standpoints.

Firstly it is most useful in observing 4QB. The Dominants immediately call out to those who perceive the picture differently, 'What! Don't be stupid!' or 'You need glasses!' It is their nature – they just have to assert. The Ds who see the other picture, argue back across the classroom. It is interesting observing the Ds run true to type.

Fig 9

Meanwhile the Is who now see both faces sit back and are amused, entertained by it and pleased they can see the two images.

The Ss who can see both, cluster round others who cannot and patiently point to where the facial features occur. You can hear them being helpful, *'Look there's the old woman's nose, follow that line, you'll see it's the young girls chin. Can you see it? No. Okay, start again....'*

Helpful, patient and cooperative. The Cs have probably deduced that there are two faces right from the beginning and can no doubt explain how such optical illusions occur.

The other benefit of the exercise is in using it to illustrate the importance of perception. At its simplest, it is where two sets of people cannot see, quite literally, the other's point of view. Imagine the situation where people not only do not see another's point of view, they won't even consider *attempting* to see that viewpoint, as can happen in Ulster.

So your perception is your reality. A GP told of a patient who wished to change doctors because she felt the GP was trying to kill her. Ludicrous and total nonsense, but her perception was her reality and much as we wish to dismiss foolish notions they first must be understood and respected.

The number of examples where perceptions differ is infinite. The police have a terrible time asking witnesses to describe an accident or a fight. Genuinely unbiased bystanders often give completely different accounts of an incident. It is also quite easy to deliberately mislead people into a false perception, for instance ask someone, *'In the Bible, how did the animals board the Ark which Moses built to save them from the flood?'* Nine out of ten will answer 'two by two'. Only the rare one (probably a C) will reply that Moses didn't build the Ark.

Another test to try is asking, *'Let me test your legal knowledge, can a man marry his widow's sister?'* Most people will pause and reply yes. Few will spot that a man cannot have a widow unless he is dead.

Simply by beginning *'How did the animals...'* or *'Let me test your knowledge of law...'*, you shift the focus of perspective away from trap.

WHO IS THE BEST TO SELL TO?

Having explained to groups the distinctness of the four psychometric types, it is interesting to ask them who is the best to sell to. Answers vary from group to group but Type-S tends to win by a short nose. Is tend to run a close second with C third and D bringing up the rear.

Why S? The response is usually on the lines that Ss are non-confrontational, helpful, caring, people-oriented and better listeners.

Why I then? Well, they are friendly, outgoing, enjoy a laugh, non-aggressive and are generally good mixers.

And why did you chose C? Because Cs are thoughtful, cool, analytical and detached. They'll weigh up your proposition and give you a careful decision.

So why did you all leave the D till last? Well, Ds are abrasive, impatient, autocratic, they interrupt, make demands and generally are not the easiest people to deal with.

The essence of perception is that nobody is wrong. But let us argue the D's case. Many would opt to negotiate with the D. You may or may not like the person but their preference is decisiveness, speed, no waffle, just do it! If they don't want your product or service, they will tell you quite quickly, there will be no evasion, justification or the dreaded, *'leave it with me for a few days, I need to think about it, I'll get back to you'*. You will be told no and it will mean No!

You can have another one or two attempts, but when Ds make a decision it is usually final. Conversely, if a D does want your product or service, you won't have to look for buying signals, or drop in *Trial Closes*, or climb the *Ladder of Yeses* or collect a number of *Naildowns*. Within quite a short time the D will ask all the key questions needed to make a decision. They also lack meanness and prefer to look at the big picture. A D characteristic is to be principled, so when they shake hands on a deal you don't have to worry too much about tying down the details of an agreement in a formally constructed contract or proposal, though it is unwise to leave everything to good faith. As the sign behind the bar puts it, *'In God We Trust – The Rest Pay Cash'*

So the Ds may not be the most pleasant to deal with but they are the quickest and the most businesslike.

The S tends to be first choice purely on account of subjective perspective. The salesperson's greatest fear is rejection. In any walk of life nobody likes being told 'no'. Consequently the S makes the human exchange more pleasant. The S will ensure you've got a coffee and maybe ask you if you found the place without any difficulty. They won't tell you to clear off or be unpleasant to you but alas, you may have to make several contacts, in person, by phone, letter or fax and though your personal relationship may be good you may not get the business. You'll probably get a sympathetic explanation as to why you're not getting the business and you may even get favourable indications that some form of future business will be pushed your way. All very civilised, but it doesn't put figures on the board.

Similarly with the I. Pleasant to sell to. Agreeable, lively and outgoing. The I actively listens and may nod a lot when you are speaking which can make you feel you are making good progress but the nods can be motivated more by a desire to be liked rather than an indication of deep comprehension of your presentation. Hard to close and if you do follow up with a phone call, you'll be treated like a long lost pal on the phone. You'll be let down easily, but a let down is still a let down.

As for Cs, yes, they are analytical. They do weigh up information and they are thorough. However, the likelihood of getting a firm decision on a first visit is remote.

Naturally it depends on the goods or services being negotiated how deeply the psychometric types manifest themselves. Some negotiations or sales can never be achieved in one visit and by their very nature are protracted. Often in business you have to deal with several people, each from a different quadrant. In the field of office equipment, you could have an initial meeting with one director who is decisive and assertive and tells you to submit a proposal to the Financial Director. The FD might be a C who will seek proposals from Rank Xerox, Konica, Minolta and Sharp or any of the leading manufacturers. He will check the specification of each, the copy cost, maintenance offered, the lease terms, the service agreements and all the minutiae of mechanical and contractual features. His eventual decision (don't rush him) will be wholly dispassionate. So even if you believe you developed a good personal relationship with the FD, that is unlikely to influence his decision to any significant degree.

QUESTIONS

Q. *Why do many psychometric systems use eight personality types?*

A. Myers-Briggs use sixteen which are permutations of Extro vert (E), Introvert (I) Thinking (T), Intuitive (N), Perceiving (P) and Judging (J) producing ESTJ, ESTP, ISTP, ISTJ, ESFJ, ESFP, ISFP, ISFJ, ENFJ, ENFP, INFP, INFJ, ENTJ, ENTP, INTP, INTJ.

Wilson Learning also use sixteen based on their DEAA – four types of Driver, four Expressives, four Amiables and four Analyticals. So each of the DEAA are themselves in four quadrants e.g. Driver Driver, Expressive Driver, Amiable Driver and Analytical Driver.

Using the painter's palette analogy, if you mix four primary colours, the permutations of shade are almost infinite. Eight, certainly is a figure in common use but once you know the basic four it is quite easy to deduce differing shades. For example you may know someone who is halfway between a C and a D (due North or Jung's Thinker). The prototype for a C/D might be a judge – someone who can absorb information analytically and then make decisions firmly and forcefully. The D/I might be a Sales Manager, someone who is a Driver yet can Inspire the sales team to achieve company targets. Analyse yourself. You will belong in one primary quadrant but you will probably lean towards one of the two adjacent to you. So you might be a caring Supporter but lean towards the cooler, detached C more than towards the more talkative and extrovert I.

Q. *Is anyone all of one quadrant?*

A. In theory it is possible to have a 4QB test result which shows someone as 100 per cent D I S or C. Granted that some people are very pronouncedly in one quadrant but in the UK many psychologists have reservations about the shorter questionnaires which isolate only the four quadrants. The example in Fig 3 is shown purely to illustrate the identification of 4QB. The benefit of the longer questionnaires such as OPQ, 16PF or RPQ (Rapid Personality Questionnaire) is in the weighting of each quality. For example RPQ might ask:

	Not **like me**			**Really** **like me**	
Forceful	1	2	3	4	5
Reserved	1	2	3	4	5
Cooperative	1	2	3	4	5
Sensitive	1	2	3	4	5

and so on. This ensures there will always be a mark for every quality. The more adjectives one is asked to weigh the more accurate the personality profile.

Q. *Is it not more precise to weigh all personality factors?*
A. If time, cost and the need for fine detail were no object, the answer has to be yes. The technical terms for two styles of test formulation are Ipsative and Normative. Ipsative tests make the individual choose between options, such as 'Are you extrovert or introvert?' or 'Are you demanding or relaxed?' From this, distinct preferences can be established. Normative tests are where questions are weighted, say on a scale of 1 to 5 and individuals are asked to ring a number on a scale of Strongly Agree to Strongly Disagree. Thus the ipsative format will deduce clearcut preferences, while the normative one will show depth or weight of certain personality traits.

6

Relationships

Loving • Marital • Personal • Professional • Sexual

In his book, *Staying Sane*, Dr Raj Persaud writes, 'Relationships with our bosses, partners, families and friends are among the most important aspects of mental health. When they are going well, we take them for granted. But if they are going badly, they become a major source of distress.'

Most people are aware to a greater or lesser degree of just how vital relationships are to our well-being and when running courses with psychometrics as a base, whether applied to sales, negotiation or management skills, someone invariably asks which quadrants make the best partners. *'In business or in personal relationships?'* I always ask.

RELATIONSHIPS – WORKING

It is easier to answer if the question relates to business partnerships. A business partnership should ideally be a balanced team. Two or three High-Cs running a business would guarantee an immaculate set of accounts, detailed reporting systems and accurate company literature. On the downside, the flair for marketing, selling and motivating the staff might be limited.

This is not speculation. An almost endless succession of High-Cs appeared on the quiz programme *Mastermind*. The contestants all had a quite extraordinary ability to not only absorb masses of information but to retrieve it in a split second. The average viewer (and non-C) could only look on in amazement. These people were truly gifted. Yet virtually every single one of the type was in a middle to low salary position. Librarians, researchers, civil servants, academics, even the unemployed. So although the preference for cerebral work and the drive to make money are not mutually exclusive, it is seldom the two qualities co-exist in the same person.

With the Is (the blind spots of the Cs) running a business, it would probably mean a happy, positive atmosphere in the workplace but attention to details such as checking invoices, stock control, running an efficient customer service department and the hundred and one repetitive tasks might be neglected to the point of rendering the business inefficient. You've probably heard many comments of this nature, *'He was a lovely guy, all his customers loved him, he was always glad to see you and have a laugh and a joke, but he had no head for business'.*

Probably he didn't lack ability or intelligence but his preference was strongly on the upper deck with the passengers when he should have had a regular look to see what went on in the engine room.

So the logic of a balanced team in business is clear. The bias will shift from industry to industry but the principle of balance remains.

POLITICAL BALANCE

The principle of balance is of course not just restricted to business. An army unit, a naval landing party, an exploring expedition or a round the world yachting crew all need balance. The need can also be observed in politics. John Major chose Jeremy Handley as PR man for the Conservative Party. The amiable Major had chosen from his own ilk. Handley was a High-I, jolly, extrovert but rather tactless and prone to gaffes with a tendency to speak when silence might have been preferable. Handley was fired and a new chairman of the party, a High-D, was selected – in theory a good choice. To balance Major's amiability, Brian Mawhinney was put in charge of winning hearts and minds. The appointment was on a par with giving King Herod the Child Welfare brief. Mawhinney was assertive and forceful. Unfortunately he proved to be rather humourless, brittle and charmless. Worse, he had a tendency to allow the 'bad day' side of the High-D to come to the fore and his displays of hostility and bad-temper on the media was one of the contributory factors to damage the image of the Tory Party. In the dying days of the Major administration, other advisors had exhorted Mawhinney to lighten up and smile a bit more. Alas, the old pitfall of acting out of character, as exemplified earlier by the Plastic D, proved just as damaging and Mawhinney's forced grin coupled with his Northern Irish accent seemed to make him more threatening rather than less.

In Jung's two hemispheres of THINKERS and FEELERS, John Major fell into the Feeling half. For balance, he tended to select people from the other hemisphere including John Redwood, Norman Lamont, Michael Portillo and Michael Howard. All of them cerebrally gifted but Major's mistake was that although such people were highly intelligent, they lacked that projection of human warmth which is absolutely vital in the winning of hearts and minds. Michael Howard in particular attracted deep opprobrium *because* of his very intelligence. When interviewed, his ability to evade a question, change it, or drown it in a deluge of complex verbiage alienated media and public alike. Both Lamont and Redwood tried to depose their benefactor, John Major, not because of any passionate dislike of the Prime Minister but because their analytical minds saw it almost as an exercise in accountancy. Redwood was even taken aback when he was attacked with emotional terms such as *back-stabber*. To the highly analytical mind, ideals such as loyalty, sportsmanship, fidelity and honour are, of course, understood but they are not a motivating force. Another example was when Redwood was Welsh Secretary. He attracted a wealth of hostile criticism for not being able to join in and sing the Welsh National Anthem. To the passionate Welsh FEELERS this was hurtful, ignorant and lacking in courtesy. To the cool THINKER, though he might grasp the logic, most of the emotion simply went over his head. Redwood was not from Major's hemisphere and caustic journalists suggested he wasn't even from the same planet.

For comparison, take Ronald Reagan. No-one could call Reagan an intellectual. His speeches were always excellent but he was a trained actor. Without his auto-cue he could be mumblingly inarticulate. It is hard to recall without a twinge of embarrassment his memorable photo-call on the White House lawn where his wife Nancy had to prompt the President of the USA on what next to say. Yet Reagan had a winning smile, he was amiable, easy, laid back, unpretentious and he made mistakes and the people liked him. In the phrase 'winning hearts and minds', it is no coincidence that hearts comes first. Jack Kennedy's famous speech with the line, *'Ask not what your country can do for you, but what you can do for your country'* is actually a piece of hollow hyperbole which doesn't stand up to intellectual analysis. But it was not intended to win minds, it was aimed directly at big, generous, patriotic, American hearts. It was a bulls-eye.

Margaret Thatcher's greatest management flair was her choice (with one or two exceptions) of a balanced team. Though she was tough and abrasive, she chose men like Geoffrey Howe, Nigel Lawson, Willie Whitelaw, Peter Carrington, Douglas Hurd and other quality people. The then Prime Minister was a singularly humourless woman (witness her famous reference to Whitelaw, *'everyone should have a Willie'*). Paradoxically, she had a good nose for a well balanced team and it was her very ability to choose such good ministers which brought about her own deposition. The Howe denunciation of Thatcher was the stuff history is made of. This S savaging a D was a text-book illustration of the S making a stand on a matter of principle. Denis Healy had once said that being attacked by Geoffrey Howe was *'like being savaged by a dead sheep.'*

Certainly Ss may seem passive but a trait of great strength in that quadrant is that they will never compromise their principles. The illustration given earlier of the High-D boss who wants to fire an employee, conflicting with a High-S Personnel Manager. They will argue in their own styles for some time but the S will win the day.

President Nixon, the High-C, suspicious and analytical, also chose a High-D as his right-hand man. Spiro Agnew was tough, strong and very assertive. Certainly Agnew helped draw some of the flak which might have been aimed at Nixon but neither was an attractive character and they made the Nixon administration one of the most unpopular this century.

The friendly, extrovert, I-type Clinton chose a good balance with the more serious C-type Al Gore, a known green and conservationist with a book published on the subject.

RELATIONSHIPS – PERSONAL

In personal relationships, it is a foolhardy observer who attempts to lay down any guidelines. For every successful combination of quadrants you might recommend, another will quote two examples of quadrant combinations which disprove the first theory. All one can do is list which seem to be the most common couplings within the four quadrant concept. Predictions of quadrant harmony are rendered virtually impossible because, whereas in team building or management consultancy the organ which makes the recommendation is the brain, in personal relationships the organ concerned is the heart.

The Heart has its reasons
which reason knows nothing of

This line penned by Blaise Pascal in the seventeenth century just about sums up the situation. Which of us has never said, *What on earth does she see in him? But they've nothing in common? He really is most unsuitable for her. She's never going out with him!* to choose only a few of the most common. So let us not enter the field of prediction – more wisely we'll take a look at some statistical evidence. Research has shown that the most common marriage match is the D/S – usually the assertive male and the caring female. Certainly it is the most common depiction in drama or fiction. No western was complete without the man's-gotta-do-what-a-man's-gotta-do male and the caring female back home at the ranch in the calico dress, who wipes flour from her hands and pinches her cheeks as her hero rides into view in a cloud of prairie dust. Clark Gable made a career out of being masterful and clasping to his manly chest females who promptly went limp on contact. Heathcliff and Cathy and a few billion pages of Mills and Boon all contribute to this match. Logically, if that is the most common imagery depicted in fiction or on stage and screen, it is reasonable to assume that is the most likely match to which people aspire. Certainly from the issue of balance it has a lot to recommend it.

However as marriage counsellors caution, it is often the strong characteristics which attracted in the first flush of love which, by their very strength, begin to irritate as complacency sets in. The S woman who found assertiveness and self assurance so attractive may, with the passage of time, find these qualities infuriating, evoking outbursts such as, *You're always right, aren't you? It doesn't occur to you you might be wrong, does it? You are so dismissive of others' views. You are so critical, intolerant, bossy ......*

The dominant male might have been captivated by his lover's passiveness, sweetness and caring qualities, but this might sour into, *Don't be so damn meek. What do you mean you don't like to make a fuss? Go back to that shop and complain like hell. You'll spoil that child.*

All quadrants can generate feelings ranging from mild irritation to downright loathing. A thoughtful C who was wildly attracted by a self-confident, extrovert I might find as time goes by that the I appears flippant, shallow and too boisterous. The C qualities of being cool, calm and collected might be a big turn-on in the beginning but may be perceived as passionless and dull as the relationship develops. For long-term stable relationships, there is considerable evidence to support same-quadrant matches. Initially, the chemistry may not be so strong as with an opposite type where the interest may even be part curiosity, *I wonder what makes her tick. He's a bit of a dark horse . I've never met anyone like her. He's so interesting.* Actually he may not be all that interesting but because he is so different, he becomes interesting.

At the risk of adding complications, one element in choosing partners should be mentioned. It is separate from psychometrics and can be called the *idée reçue* or accepted idea. This lyric from the wartime song expresses this very well,

> *I want a girl, just like the girl,*
> *who married dear old Dad.*

How old-fashioned that seems now, but you get the drift. There are men who make a fuss because their partners do not do things the way mother did. A further complication is *over-rejection* of the accepted idea such as the daughter of an old-fashioned disciplinarian father. She chooses a man who is sweet, kind, considerate and helpful about the house. Her wish is to shake off all the unhappy memories of dominance, discipline and disapproval. Alas, the *idée reçue* may be so imbedded that she finds her partner characterless and wishy-washy. Also by trying to mask the bad times with her autocratic father, she may also forget the good times associated with his authoritarian manner such as his stalwartness, his certainty or his protectiveness in standing up for his daughter against some injustice. And although her lover may be the epitome of attentiveness and care, her *accepted idea* of how a man should be may be so deep as to create serious problems with her relationship.

SHARED INTERESTS

With same quadrant relationships, the special cement of good partnerships – shared interests – can develop. The High-S wife who is happiest at home, married to a High-I who loves to be in the pub may well enjoy a happy and long term match, but the dangers are inherent in their preferences. Two High-Cs who holiday on an archaeological dig may not sound as attractive as Club Med types to some but the ability to share such a deep and specialist interest augurs well for a long and contented future.

Years ago, I never understood why I disliked the company of teachers so much. Not teacher in the singular, but teachers. On a one-to-one basis, I enjoyed the company of teacher friends. On reflection I now can see they were mainly Ss. We could philosophise and solve the problems of the world. Being generally well educated, their subject range was wide and the exchange usually satisfying and stimulating. While all professions tend to talk shop, when two or more teachers were in company, their propensity to discuss the day's events was total. Who said what to whom in the staff room, the stupidity of the new curriculum, the cut-backs in budget, the types of kids, the types of parents, the head, the deputy head and so on ad infinitum – out it all came. They do not intend to be rude to any unfortunate non-teachers in the company, they just cannot help it. When they would congregate it was clearly time to leave. They, being S-types took no offence and in fairness, most teachers recognise this weakness in the profession. Quite a high proportion of teachers marry teachers.

The problem area for same quadrant relationships is two

High-Ds. In any situation there may be friction between two High-Ds. If the preference is for assertion, authoritativeness and autocracy, life can be difficult for two of the same disposition. The word *auto* is from the Greek for *self* and where self is a preference, it may make loving, giving, caring, consideration and tolerance more difficult than in another quadrant. We all know the descriptions, *They had a stormy marriage. They fought like cat and dog. She would storm out of one door and he out of another. They could break an entire dinner service between them. You could hear them three blocks away* .

It is a fair bet that these two are High Ds. This volatile picture is often balanced with, *But they always came back to each other. They just had to have one another.*

Charles Handy, in his book, *The Age of Unreason,* carried out some research on quadrant matches. He incidentally identified the four types as THRUSTERS, INVOLVED, CARING & LONERS. These are his words but they dovetail perfectly with all the other terms used by psychometricians from Hippocrates onwards. Handy points out that there are sixteen different possible combinations but by far the most common combination was the THRUSTING male and the CARING female or our D/S.

His research concluded the most common matches as,

1. THRUSTING male with a CARING female
2. Two INVOLVEDS
3. Two LONERS
4. Two THRUSTERS

The reference to Geoffrey Howe's famous savaging of Margaret Thatcher in a prepared speech in the House of Commons is worth extrapolating into the field of D/S personal relationships. An interesting aspect of homicide is found in the cases of husbands being murdered by wives. A relatively modern development in criminal justice is the number of cases where a woman walks free from a court having murdered a tyrant of a husband. This is frequently where a High-D male (possibly with a low IQ or some form of inadequacy) allows his natural bent for assertion to develop into aggression and then deteriorate into violence. The High-S female whose disposition is towards harmony, non-confrontation and passiveness may allow this destructive situation to continue over time. But the High-S will sooner or later take a stand on her principles and prove quite resolute. The Howe attack on Thatcher was breathtaking and historic not so much for the strength of its language but the fact it was delivered by Howe (or Denis Healy's *dead sheep*). So with the battered wife, when she decides enough and no more, her strength of resolve can be overwhelming. Those who have not considered psychometric types and the consistency of 4QB often comment, *She was so quiet. She was a good neighbour, always ready to help. She wouldn't say boo to a goose. She was so good to the kids. I just can't imagine her hurting a fly.*

The corollary of these comments is that the act of murder, especially violent murder, is more in keeping with a High-D or someone with pronounced assertiveness and a fiery temper.

This is bad logic. The woman with a fiery temper or from the High-D quadrant would never have allowed a pattern of abuse, verbal or physical, to develop in the first place. The male who crosses the High-D woman will be under no illusion as to how much she resents it. The press is full of stories of women who have cut the crotches from their men's trousers, sold the BMW for pennies, poured his prized wine collection down the drain or, in the notorious Bobbit case, removed the offending body part with a sharp implement. The main reason for the worldwide notoriety of this latter case was because it sent a frisson of fear through the entire brotherhood of man.

So, although the act of homicide might seem more consistent with the D quadrant, it is often the S female who has endured more than she is prepared to take. The High-D just does not tolerate the intolerable. Also the bullying male is often a coward and when confronted with fiery resistance he tends to mend his ways.

RELATIONSHIPS – LOVING

Let us continue with the sweeter subject of love and Pascal's observation that love doesn't reason. Thankfully, in western society, we choose our partners through that part of the brain which dictates our emotions. Otherwise we'd all have arranged marriages which would include a psychometric test.

The only view of love and marriage from a psychometric standpoint has to be a retrospective one. We can only look back and observe the quadrant balances which have worked best in the past. Even then you can only reach a statistical predominance or indicator. There can be no outright formulae.

Computer dating is an attractive idea. Load in dossiers of information about men and women and let the machine make the match. At best it will help avoid matching an Israeli freedom fighter with Yasser Arafat's niece but love makes its own rules. Sustaining love is another matter. Like all relationships, what you obtain from it depends on what you put in it. Even with all the right ingredients it is like a fire. It won't burn on its own forever. It needs tending, with a regular supply of solid fuel fed to it. Looked after, it need never go out but neglect it or take it for granted or assume someone else will do all the work and however bright the flame may have been it may just flicker and die.

PHYSICAL ATTRACTION AND SEXUAL ATTRACTION

These might appear to be twins but they are only first cousins. We all have recognised great physical attractions in people but when it comes to the clinch, the sexual chemistry may not sparkle as expected. Men are less complex than women and often find little distinction between the two but women are quite emphatic about what constitutes one and where the other is a real turn-on. These reactions are intensely personal and seldom can two people agree on them. In so saying and as a movie enthusiast, forgive me if I indulge the personal. Physically striking stars such as Katherine Hepburn, Bo Derek, Jamie Lee Curtis and Margaux Hemingway all could evoke admiration for their sheer physical beauty but, for me, there was no sex appeal. With the latter two, perhaps because I knew the male lineage of Tony Curtis and Ernest Hemingway, it may have clouded my subconscious image with male genes which proved a turn-off. Who knows? You can actually play this as a party game. Who is beautiful and a turn-off and who is not physically attractive yet a turn-on? Disagreement guaranteed.

After my mother had been to see the movie *Dr Zhivago*, I asked her how she had enjoyed it and what had she thought of the then heartthrob Omar Sharif. She dismissed the dishy Omar with a few curt phrases and added, *'But that Rod Steiger, now he was really something!'* Short, portly Steiger was in an unpleasant role, but mother was giving him five stars for sex appeal while Sharif got the thumbs down.

Physical attractiveness is all about a symmetry of profile or shape, an aesthetically pleasing form or combination of colouring or texture of skin or hair. Sex appeal is something else. Love at first sight sounds like a form of lunacy but although the actual love might not be kindled with the first eyeful, all the ingredients which contribute to this passion may exist.

The best lyric writers have all had something to say on this issue.

Some enchanted evening you may see a stranger.
Nancy with the laughing face.
You see a pair of laughing eyes.
The minute you walked in the joint.
The more I see you, the more I want you.
They way you wear your hat, the way you sip your tea.
With your long blonde hair and your eyes of blue.
Something in the way he moves.
Oh Spanish eyes.
Just one look, that's all it took.

Romantic lyrics have a recurrent list of body parts which never include the bits we might be forgiven for having a healthy interest in. Eyes seem to top the attraction charts, then smile, lips, teeth, nose, hair, chin, movement and overall aura. Ears are not too prominent unless they are just that.

No romantic lyricist has yet penned such an immortal line as, *You are the psychometric quadrant for me.*

Apart from the physical, a brief scan of the lonely-hearts column will confirm the priorities of the male and female. Though men seem to be more subtle than they used to be, they still appear to place value on the physically attractive raver, whereas women constantly seek a good sense of humour – so consistently that it is now abbreviated to GSOH – and qualities such as caring and consideration.

Love can exist in any combination of quadrants. All psycho-metrics can do is help you to understand why certain aspects of a partner can be so important or so irritating as the case may be. Conversely, in an apparently good quadrant match with phys-ical and sexual attraction, that elusive quality of love can fail to develop. However with so much going for it, it might be fun trying. The absence of love in a union is more likely to cause grief than a quadrant mismatch. Analysts of the Charles and Diana marriage often identified their differences. He was from Jung's northern hemisphere, the Thinkers, while she was very much from the southern hemisphere, the Feelers. As she lost her shyness, she developed into an excellent communicator, warm, friendly and extrovert. Observers claimed he became jealous of her as he became more typecast as the detached and analytical C. Certainly the I/C combo is normally better in a Male/Female context rather than Female/Male because men can be petulant if the wife seems to lead and sparkle. But this was not the root of the problem. The root was simply that he did not love her. With a completely open heart, love can develop as it often does in arranged marriages. This famous marriage was doomed because his heart was not open – he already loved another. All of us hate rejection but the I-type suffers most from it and Diana was about 60/40 S/I. One of the reasons the sympathy felt for this woman was so overpowering was that fifty percent of the population (the Feelers) could identify totally with her and the other half, if less emotional, could at least understand it.

ASTROLOGY AND FAITH

Given the amount of time people pore over the astrological predictions in the newspapers, it is fair to assume that many people consider it important to be able to categorise a human being. Every daily tabloid newspaper carries a horoscope column and even some of the quality broadsheets have adopted the practice. There is not a person in western society who does not know their own star sign. Even those who are most sceptical about astrology know which sign of the Zodiac they come under.

So we can deduce that people consider it important to be able to quantify characteristics and traits in themselves and others. Just why they should choose to place any faith in such an idiotic system is totally mystifying. Perhaps the very lack of scientific or empirical evidence to support such nonsense is what perpetuates the interest in it. Four quadrant behaviour is a far more useful tool in gauging people. It also has the merits of being clearly observable, consistent, proven and simple. Perhaps it was Jung's terminology which put the general public off. Certainly it is easier to say, *She was a typical Virgo* rather than *He was a classic Extroverted Intuitive Thinker*.

This is where animal identification could have been universally useful. If quadrants were classified as LIONS, DOLPHINS, LABRADORS and OWLS, after a brief study of psychometrics, the whole world could talk, for example, of,

A Typical Dolphin – playful, fun-loving extrovert or
A Classic owl – quiet, reserved, thoughtful.

Insights International Ltd of Dundee use an excellent colour based system. Instead of the most common 4QB identifiers, DISC, for DOMINANTS, INSPIRERS, SUPPORTERS and COORDINATORS, they use Red, Yellow, Green and Blue. These colours have natural associations red for a fiery temperament; yellow for sunshine; green for the carers; and blue for the cool, detached, analytical types. The benefit of colours is that they are neutral and non-judgemental. Words like Drivers, Dominants, Supporters or Detached all have varying connotations for people whereas colours are just colours.

Despite these excellent methods of simplifying the infinitely more accurate and intelligent concept of 4QB, it never acquired broad appeal, so large numbers of people still look to astrology.

7

Selling

In my book, *Close More Sales*, I looked at the sales cycle in detail, taking the selling process step by step through the stages of:

Developing the Correct Attitude
Why People Buy
Understanding the Numbers Game
The Cash Value of Each Contact
Suspects & Prospects
Approaching – By Phone, Mailshot or Cold Calling
The Sales Interview
Probing, Listening, Naildowns, Trial Closes
Closing the Sale

This is the basic tool kit. Successful salespeople will be equipped with these tools and a sound grasp of how they are used.

In the book, some mention was made of the buyer, but little attempt was made to describe the psychological disposition of the four base psychometric types and, by extension, no mention could be made of the psychological interaction between buyer and seller.

USING 4QB IN SELLING

For every selling exercise taking place there is also a buying exercise. Years ago sales trainers developed the *spiel*. Just deliver it parrot-fashion and you'd make the sales. While there is a sound argument for having a presentation format, the old school made no allowance for the personality type of both the seller and the buyer. A wham-bam-thank-you-ma'am delivery might suit a High-D seller but a High-S would recoil from it. A glowing verbal picture-painting sales presentation might suit a High-I but the High-C would not be happy with it. Similarly, from the point of view of the *buyer*, not only must your sales pitch match the buyer's needs but your *style* of presentation should suit his personality type. Personality types can be gauged quite early on during the introductions or when putting the *goalposts* (see page 122) in place.

Careful application of these principles can make a huge difference to sales results, as is often confirmed by the many salespeople I have trained over the years. When delegates on my sales courses first come to grips with the 4QB element, it is fascinating to observe their recognition as they begin to identify the four distinct types that they have dealt with, and place themselves in the appropriate quadrant relative to the buyer.

It is particularly rewarding, as the delegates typically already possess the basic toolkit and many have been selling for years. Often, their initial attitude is cool, with an undercurrent of *what can this guy teach me?* But this soon changes as the message sinks home.

The first and most obvious benefit for the sales force is that 4QB gives them a common language, and a framework to analyse past successes and failures. Once delegates grasp the basics, they begin to give examples of sales interviews they have experienced, such as this cable salesman.

'I was with this classic High-S last night. Lovely woman, offered me a cup of tea, asked where I came from, how I liked my job. Chat, I

thought she'd never shut up. And when I got onto the subject of TV choice she started on about the different soaps, the characters, the relationships, the lot. An hour and a half I was with her.'
    'Did you get the sale?"
    'Don't ask.'

Another salesman described his experience:

'I had a one hundred percent C yesterday. Got his last four phone bills out and wanted to compare about twenty BT prices against the cable rates, then added in line rental. Even took my calculator from me and did all the sums himself. As soon as I answered one question, he was asking another. Finally agreed cable was cheaper – so I asked him for the order. Do you know what he said to me?'
    'No. tell me.'
    'He said, "I want to think about it"!'

An important part of the exercise is getting the salespeople to identify which quadrant they belong to themselves. They generally grow quite enthusiastic about this and enjoy recognising the traits in themselves and in their colleagues. One delegate had the nick-name 'The Piranha'. In the field he took no prisoners. He was quick, to the point, incisive, closed hard and had little time for unnecessary talk. As you might have guessed he was a High-D.

In the Introduction to this book I mentioned my conversion to both the value and the accuracy of these tests. Their accuracy has been borne out by the hundreds of delegates who have undergone psychometric tests as part of my courses. Not one disagreed with the quadrant in which they were placed, and I am often greeted by comments such as *'Oh, that's me to a T'*, or (to another delegate) *'Yes, that's typical of you'*. Remember it is their own view, their self-assessment and they mark the test results themselves. Had an outside party tried to tell the people which type they were, the acceptance might have been less comprehensive. Many accepted the quadrant in which they were placed but claimed to have strong influences from other quadrants. Perfectly natural. No-one is all D, I, S or C – quite the reverse as all of us are a mixture of all four quadrants but all of us have one strongest *preference* or gift.

By understanding the types in 4QB and by placing yourself in the correct quadrant, it then becomes easy to examine why, in a given sales situation (or any other situation) human interaction can either be harmonious or uncomfortable – and why you did or did not get on with a manager, a colleague, a teacher, a relative or anyone with whom regular contact is made.

BLIND SPOTS

The quadrant which is diametrically opposite your own is said to be your *Blind Spot*. If you are a NORTH EASTER you will feel comfortable with other NEs. You will also be able to communicate reasonably well with those from the quadrants either side of you, the analytical NWs and the buoyant SEs. The *Blind Spot* for the NE is the SW where communication can be difficult and at times impossible. The typical communication difficulty is where the SW from personnel needs to discuss some compassionate element of staff handling with a NE senior manager. Not only is the NE predisposed to be abrupt, impatient and even intolerant, but faced with a SW style of presentation, it will bring out the worst in him and he'll attack the submission as being *soft*, or *giving in to the staff* or *what more do they want!* More likely, communication will break down altogether.

This is a classic scenario in the old war movies. The humanitarian middle ranker appeals to his superior,

'Sir, the men need a break.'
'Nonsense!'
'Sir, they've been holed up in this God-forsaken place for six months now. No leave, no wives, no girl-friends, no recreation, just

route-marches, assault training and the heat.'

'Tough, Lieutenant. This is a man's army. We don't want them getting soft.'

'But, sir...'

'Beat it, Lieutenant. That's an order.'

You've seen it in many forms. It is probable that the Dominant is more flexible but because he sees his *Blind Spot* as a bleeding heart, he becomes more resolute, to the detriment of the people on whose behalf the S-Type was interceding. The reverse is the situation given earlier where the High-D manager wants to fire an employee or two and finds an implacable personnel manager of the S disposition who will not hear of someone being summarily dismissed and insists on a whole raft of procedures being adhered to. This frustrates the D to the point of explosion. His whole nature is 'Do it and do it now!'. He wants action and sees any compromise or delay as giving in and defeatist. The D/S conflict can cause turmoil within an organisation because the D is autocratic and the S will die for his principles. The S may not be assertive or aggressive but qualities like loyalty and duty rank high with him. Although the S may argue his case in a civilised manner and even appear rather passive, this should never be mistaken for submissiveness. On a matter of principle, the S tends not to give in.

The C and the I are perhaps more obvious *Blind Spots* for each other. Obvious in every sense; the C is cool, detached, analytical while the I is impulsive, loud and outgoing. The big box office success movie, *The Odd Couple* focused on this quite simple theme and the spin-off TV series was equally successful. In the movie, Jack Lemmon played the divorced C who moved in with his old pal Walter Matthau, the long divorced and party-loving I, a slob who likes to have his pals in to play poker, drink beer, smoke cigars and eat sandwiches, producing that famous line, *'What sort of sandwiches ya got?'* Walter lifts the bread to examine the contents, *'I got red ones and I got green ones.'*

The C on the other hand likes things neat. He wants to tidy

up the kitchen, do the shopping, plan dinner and be organised.

Pretty simple stuff but – good acting and a good script aside – we all recognised the situation with greater or lesser degrees of identification; the Cs and Is totally, while the Ds and Ss were close enough to empathise sufficiently with the characterisation.

With no knowledge of psychometric types, when we encounter *Blind Spots* we will probably just generalise – *I didn't like the guy. I just couldn't get on with her. Not my type/cup of tea. She wasn't on my frequency/wavelength. We were poles apart.*

It is interesting how accurate the 'poles apart' phrase is from a psychometric standpoint. One major advantage of understanding 4QB is that it helps to explain these kinds of Blind-Spot encounters (and failures), and by rationalising to dispell sensations of anger, frustration and confusion. It can also enable us to vary our methods and presentation according to our own quadrant and that of the prospect in order to achieve a positive outcome.

SELLING YOURSELF – THE JOB INTERVIEW

Take the standard job interview, a sale we all have to make. It is not too difficult to deduce the quadrant of the interviewer quite early on, even at the greeting stage. The way you are invited into the room, the words used, the manner, the facial expression, the body language, the hospitality offered (or lack of it), the questions asked, the eye contact, the manner with which the questions are asked and so on. All these indicators can very quickly show the quadrant of the person. This then can help remove several of the post-interview frustrations, such as, *He didn't seem interested in a word I said. All the preparatory work I put in, and she just didn't want to know.*

Granted you cannot change your own quadrant, but you can play up or play down certain aspects of your character or achievement to suit the type of interviewer.

If the interviewer is a High-C, there is little point in

enthusing about hobbies and your love of the local amateur dramatic group or how much you enjoy a good karaoke evening. And if you are a great team player and love working with other people, this may not be on top of the C's list of priorities. Being too eager to answer a question or replying with too much enthusiasm may overpower the C. On the other hand an ebullient, talkative and extrovert interviewer may take to your people-orientation immediately.

In a sales vacancy interview, the veteran salesman applicant will often relate how numbers-oriented he is and how he can deliver a wham-bam-thank-you-ma'am presentation, close the deal and move smartly on to the next sale. A tough-minded sales manager may respond favourably to this and think this is just what we need. However, if the initial interview is conducted by a High-S from personnel, the S's response might be to consider the applicant brash, uncaring and unattractive.

The problem with interviews is that we often prepare thoroughly, listing all our achievements and good qualities, and we are determined to get these factors across no matter what. Our anxiety to deliver our *pitch* eclipses our need to observe the type we are talking to. Like a good song, it can be delivered to a rag-time beat or a blues tempo or up or down tempo to suit the audience. Or you can have a repertoire of songs where you leave one out or add one, depending on the mood and venue.

SELLING A PRODUCT OR SERVICE

The four components of any sale are that you sell:

1. Yourself
2. Your Company
3. Your Product or Service
4. Your Price

Of the four components, it could be argued that the most

important is your product or service because that is what the customer actually buys. Quite fair, but you may not get the opportunity to present your product unless you first make sale No 1 – yourself.

Ask yourself, how many stores have you walked out of with the intended purchase still firmly in your mind and your money still firmly in your pocket, simply because you did not like the manner of the sales assistant. You, the buyer, walked purposefully into a store with a specific purchase in mind and cash in your pocket, yet you turned round and walked out without the item you actually had decided to buy because you did not like an individual's manner. The store would probably have made the sale had it switched to self-service and not employed the sales assistant in the first place. Three out of the four stages were already 'sold' – you walked into the store happy with the *Company*, *Product* and *Price*. But the sale still failed because of the salesperson's failure to sell themselves.

It is obviously even more important as a salesperson to sell yourself where the prospective buyer has really no firm intention of buying but just agrees to see you out of curiosity or even out of professional courtesy, just to give the seller a chance to make a presentation.

There are six components which can determine the success or failure of a salesperson (Fig 10). Assuming you are selling in a business environment as opposed to a domestic one, these six ingredients are expressed as slices in a pie-chart. As the chart shows, by far the largest slice relates to the personality and attitude of the salesperson – the very area where an understanding of psychometrics can offer invaluable assistance.

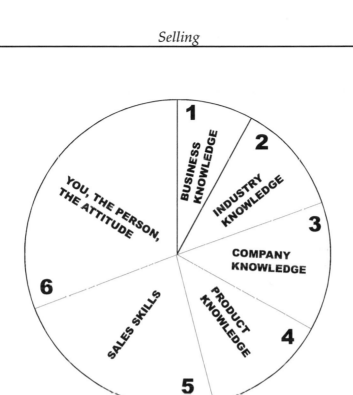

Fig 10. The Circle of Success

WHAT MAKES THE IDEAL SALES REP?

Some sales organisations deliberately recruit High-Ds. Thomas International, one of the main players in the field of psycho-metrics, prefer the High-Ds to sell their own services. They know that selling is a numbers game, and that the Ds are more hard-nosed and pragmatic and less likely to let rejection bother them. Their understanding of 4QB tells them that High-I is often great when in front of a prospect but tends to take rejection badly and lacks the sheer determination to drive on to achieve the necessary key ratios. One term for the D quadrant is just that – *Drivers....*

On the other hand, managers *interviewing* for salespeople generally have preference for High-Is because the Inspirer is good at interviews and the manager is predisposed to 'buy' from him. Job applicants know that the easy bit is the interview stage. A facet of the High-I personality is a tendency to be easily distracted and the need to be acknowledged. Thomas International are fully aware of this and know the risks of recruiting High-I people in sales, as the rejection rate will eventually be too much for them. The High-S is similarly vulnerable and the High-C, though more self-contained and analytical, often lacks the presence to inspire the prospect to buy.

THE RECRUITER'S DILEMMA

Advertisements for salespeople often use words like *self-reliant, self-starter, with initiative, independent, creative,* etc. (Invariably the description of a High-I). In recruiting people with these qualities employers should be aware that this kind of recruit is likely to be unsympathetic to wards excessively rigorous reporting requirements, such as:

> *How many telephone calls have you made?*
> *How many got past the receptionist?*
> *How many decision-makers did you speak to?*
> *How many appointments did you make?*
> *How many call-backs?*
> *How many mailshots sent?*
> *How many appointed visits did you make?*
> *How many cold-call visits?*
> *How many interviews/presentations?...*

If extensive reporting procedures are required, employers should be careful to recruit representatives with the right personality profile to deal with this.

Otherwise, as happens in all too many a company today,

employers may find salespeople 'feeding the beast' – fabricating reports (starting with the actual number of orders and working backwards 'creatively' to produce the desired ratios) in order to produce the required paperwork, which is, of course, meaningless. In psychometric terms, Expressives have been recruited but given the reporting system for Analyticals...

HIGH-Cs AND SALES PERFORMANCE RATIOS

Every rep has to know his ratios – how many prospects they are converting, what proportion of sales they are closing, and how the value of their sales relates to their costs. High-Cs are particularly adept at this.

Years ago one of the top and most consistent earners in financial services sales told me that every time he picked up the phone it earned him £3.68 in commission. He knew to the penny what his ratios were. One hundred Suspect call would ultimately produce £368 in commission. On a day when he produced no business he would check his call-sheet, see he had made 25 calls and say 'I've earned £92 today.' He was very much a High-C, an accurate record-keeper and very stoical about key ratios. Also, his analytical preference allowed him to present financial packages with professionalism and credibility.

SELLING A BUSINESS PLAN

Everyone starting out in business, whether in a small retail shop or a middle-sized manufacturing unit, has to produce a Business Plan. No bank manager will even consider supporting a new venture without seeing an intelligently compiled Business Plan with a well thought out cash flow projection. The bank manager will quiz the new entrepreneur on detail after detail contained in the plan. The High-I will present his business plan with enthusiasm and gusto but he may come apart on the minutiae of the figures whereas the High-C might be able to account for every penny of his plan but fall down in the area of imbuing the bank with confidence of success. The truth is that a successful presentation requires a combination of both.

Often partners in business join together because of like-mindedness. Two High-Is might be great visionaries full of PMA (Positive Mental Attitude) and brimming with enthu-siasm. Though they like each other's positiveness of attitude, as a partnership it might well be more prudent to have a blind-spot partner to create a more balanced team. Rather like a Dom-inant chairman who has a subservient board of directors, there is minimal disagreement and only one perspective. For flame you need friction.

GOALPOSTS

No competent meeting should take place without an agenda. Similarly, in sales, the flow of the exchange is much smoother when goalposts are in place. But try to ascertain the 4QB char-acteristics before setting your goalposts in stone. The introduc-tions will give you a chance to start to evaluate the customer's profile, and this process should continue right up to the point at which the final agenda is set.

Goalposts are particularly valuable when selling to a High-D whose preference is to assert, interrupt and take charge. If you can lay out your agenda or goalposts, you are less likely to be put under pressure by the Dominant buyer. In financial ser-vices sales the salesperson would begin, *'In order to establish the most suitable package for you, I need to know something about your circumstances, so I'd like to begin by asking you a few standard ques-tions, if I may.'*

Having gained agreement, the salesperson is then free to kick-off, so he produces his Fact Find form and can build up a quite comprehensive profile of the potential client. If the seller began without placing goalposts and simply went ahead with a series of personal questions, the buyer can feel resentful, interrupt and decide to take charge of the interview.

The seller can not only put down the goalposts but can also give an indication of the direction of play. Once the buyer nods approval the seller is free to travel the route of questions outlined. This overcomes the risk of beginning by firing a series of questions at the buyer, who by about question five or six is starting to feel a little brow-beaten.

The salesperson simply follows the tried, tested and perfectly logical structure – goalposts first, then...

STRUCTURE

As every rep knows, good selling is all about a methodical structure – a logical sequence of steps which will take you from introduction through to close... But it is important to adopt a structure which has the flexibility to be modified according to the 4QB characteristics of both seller and customer. The IDEA/FAB structure works as follows:

1. **Gain all the relevant INFORMATION**
2. **Probe for areas of DISSATISFACTION**
3. **Probe for all the EFFECTS of the dissatisfaction**
4. **Gain AGREEMENT that improvement is needed**
5. **Now you may sell the FEATURES, ADVANTAGES & BENEFITS of your product.**

One advantage of this framework is that each step can be accomplished in a number of different ways, according to the personality types involved. For example a High-C car-buyer will have thoroughly researched his purchase already; the best way to obtain information from him will be to ask what he knows, and if you can add or correct any technical information you are on the right wavelength. The Is and Ss, on the other hand, may well volunteer the whole story for the seller and give the car's life story, interspersed with colourful detail and all the seller has to do is actively listen, making sympathetic noises and giving a gentle nudge here and there to keep the flow of information coming.

Also, the steps can be accomplished in a different order. For example, a High-C car buyer might begin by saying that she has decided to change her car. So we're already at **A** for Agreement that it is time to change. Why does she want to change? And we are at **D** for Dissatisfaction without probing for any Information. Similarly a High-D car buyer might be a *tyre-kicker* who demands, *How much is this? How much discount can you give me on this? How much will you give me for this?* In this case you are taken straight to **FAB** and have to fill in the other stages as best you can...

As long as all parts of the IDEA/FAB approach are addressed the sale can be achieved. In some circumstances, the seller might never get fluently into the structure, but it is always there as a guide. It may even be counterproductive to stick to the IDEA structure too rigidly. A common cliche in sales is that we have two ears and one mouth and should use them in that ratio. Forcing a line of questions in a given structure is a prime example of ignoring this ratio.

QUESTIONS FOR THINKERS AND FEELERS

There are many different kinds of question that can be used in steering a prospect towards a sale:

Closed questions
Open questions
Reflective questions
Leading questions
Rhetorical questions
Multiple questions

Closed questions are questions which can be answered with just a 'yes' or a 'no', such as 'Would you like to try this out?' They are not particularly good at eliciting information but can be helpful in steering a prospect along a predetermined path. They can be particularly useful when dealing with High-Is or High-Ss (Jung's *Feelers)* who may be apt to stray from the point.

Open questions are questions that cannot be answered with just a 'yes' or a 'no', but require an explanation or a point of view – for example 'what do you particularly like about this product?' Their principal purpose is to obtain information (the **I** of IDEA). In the words of Rudyard Kipling:

> *I had six serving men,*
> *They taught me all I knew.*
> *Their names were WHAT and WHY and WHEN*
> *And HOW and WHERE and WHO.*

Open questions always begin with one of Kipling's six. As well as procuring information they allow a conversation to flow. They are particularly useful when selling to a High-D or High-C (Jung's *Thinkers).* If you ask a *Thinker* if they like something, they may well respond with a yes or no and leave it at that; ask them *why* they like it, and you will learn something useful.

The **reflective question** is self-explanatory. One simply reflects back something said by the other person,

> *'We had that make of car once but we got rid of it.'*
> *'Rid of it?'*
> *'Yes, it gave us nothing but trouble, most unreliable.'*
> *'Unreliable?'*
> *'Too right, if was off the road more than on.'*

Reflective questions are especially useful in keeping a flow of information going. They are not intrusive. They are not judgemental. They are not distracting and keep the speaker's mind on the subject. Be careful about constantly repeating back the last word or two, though. If overdone, someone might enquire if there is a parrot in the room.

The other version of a reflective question is simply to make a reflective or thoughtful noise, such as Oh?, Yeah? or Really? following the buyer's statement. This is unintrusive, sympathetic and keeps the flow going without danger of 'parroting'.

Leading questions are Trial Closes, *'So you've made up your mind to change then?' 'So you've decided to cut your losses then?'*

Rhetorical questions are simply pieces of rhetoric which need no answer, *'That's the last thing you want, isn't it.' 'You could do without the hassle, couldn't you?'*

In selling, a **multiple question** is often hugely effective in getting the IDEA ball rolling. *'You want to look at some golf clubs. Right, to help me advise you properly, could you just give me a brief overview on details such as how long you've been playing, how often you play, if you have a handicap, what you've been used to, what sort of price range, that sort of thing...'* – a lovely big juicy multiple question which deserves a big juicy answer. The seller can then actively listen, nodding, making the odd reflective noise or throwing in the odd reflective question. The multiple question is useful for the *Thinkers*. The *Feelers* may well tell you their life story without prompting.

A multiple question shouldn't be confused with asking too many questions at once which could confuse or irritate the buyer, it is simply a guide to the range of information required.

CASE STUDIES

a. 'He was so rude and abrupt. Wouldn't let me finish a sentence...'

b. 'Nice guy, friendly, full of fun, but I just couldn't tie him down.'

c. 'Lovely woman, hospitable, asked lots of questions, introduced me to others, but I just could not get an order.'

d. 'Cold fish, long silences, wanted everything in writing,
   wanted proof of everything...'

All salespeople recognise these phrases. The less experienced
might blame themselves. What did I do wrong? Often there
was nothing done wrong; it was 4QB at work. The a. is
assertive, the b. buoyant, the c. caring and the d. detached, all
running true to type.

8

Negotiation

It could be argued that negotiation and selling belong in the same chapter but negotiation covers a much broader band of human exchange. From Mo Mowlam conferring with David Trimble and Gerry Adams to the ten year old son of the house who innocently says, Dad, the car could do with a wash, negotiation is the pursuit of a satisfactory settlement. Negotiation takes place in some form on a daily basis. When we marry, we negotiate. How many guests; civil ceremony or church; which church; who to include; who to leave out and a lengthy list which has to be acceptable to both parties and often both families. When we divorce, we negotiate – the heartbreaking negotiation of dividing the very symbols of the union. We negotiate when we buy a house, change car, seek a pay rise, plan a holiday or decide on whether to invite a certain relative for Christmas. Our speech is riddled with the language of negotiation, *on one condition; providing that; only if; I'm prepared to do that if; what's in it for me? let's compromise* .... and many more.

To illustrate John Adair's three circles, Task, Team & Individual in Chapter 4, we looked at the task of the family planning a holiday and how one individual made a selfish decision to the detriment of both the team and the task. If mum wants sun and a touch of sophistication, the kids want fun and excitement and dad wants a level of tranquillity, *nobody is going to get one hundred per cent of what they want*. That understanding is the very core of understanding the principles of negotiation. The skill lies in achieving the maximum percentage for all. And to do this, it is essential to understand what drives each party at the table.

This is where psychometrics come in. If you are able to identify the 4QB types involved in any given negotiation you will hold the key not only to their attitudes and styles of negotiation, but also to the priorities and objectives which will determine their position as the negotiation develops.

DOMINATION, CONFRONTATION OR NEGOTIATION

Parties who have differing interests but who need to reach a common solution face three options:

DOMINATION
CONFRONTATION
NEGOTIATION

In each of these areas, psychometrics has a role to play – whether for purposes of avoidance or mitigation (the first two), or in making the most of a full-blown negotiation.

Domination

Domination is the resort of the High-D – but only when the other parties to the negotiation will let him (or her) get away with it! The resentment it creates can make it a dangerous strategy, even when the initial decision goes the dominator's way. Whilst the approach might work with High-Cs and even with some Is and Ss it is a recipe for disaster when applied to other Ds. And, as most reasonable people know, it does not form a basis for lasting co-operation in any but the most disciplinarian environments (the army for one; the Houses of Parliament for another).

In management terms, the dominant approach with little or no room for negotiation is, thankfully, dying out. This style of management was identified by McGregor as the 'X' style where workers clocked-on, were given little scope for initiative and worked at a given pace on a given task. The 'Y' style where objectives are agreed and workers are left to achieve those objectives is now the norm. Surprisingly the 'Y' style was adopted most vigorously by the people who in society were accustomed to hierarchical structures, the Japanese. Though there were one or two British pioneers of the 'Y' style, Britain clung very much to the 'X' variation, partly due to its strong military heritage and partly because of the rigid class system. One notable exception was Wilfred Taylor, MD of London-based Glacier Metal. As early as the 1950s, he and Canadian psychologist Elliott Jacques, began to introduce the 'Y' style concept. Taylor considered clocking-on degrading and found giving trust and respect to his workforce evoked more cooperation and loyalty than the traditional autocratic style. One of the reasons the military today finds it so difficult to recruit good calibre personnel is because of its adherence to the 'X' style of management along with its reluctance to distance itself from the entrenched class divisions of the past. Being granted unquestioning obedience has a place in the military but the *'you're not paid to think, laddie'* attitude will not work with today's young people.

If you are a High-D, inclined to dominate rather than negotiate, try a more conciliatory approach: you will be surprised at the results. If, on the other hand, you find yourself on the receiving end of a dominant approach, try playing them at their own game, using the techniques referred to on page 137. If you are able to gain their respect as an adversary you may persuade them to negotiate rather than dictate. If this doesn't work, walk away!

Confrontation

Negotiation can often break down not because of an absolute clash of ideology or positions, but because of a conflict of *Blind Spots* (see page 114 above), where negotiators in one 4QB type come up against negotiators in the opposite type and fail to make the necessary adjustments. Some of the fiercest political clashes in recent times were between John Major and Ian Paisley. Using the four psychometric descriptions, *Dominant, Expressive, Amiable* and *Analytical,* Paisley was very much the Dominant while Major was from the Amiable quadrant. When *Amiables* stand their ground they can be quite resolute.

Sometimes the situation itself can lead to confrontation, particularly where there is a lack of preparation on either part. However, it often boils down to just a question of personalities. It is well known that once a confrontation develops it is hard to defuse it; the best solution is to anticipate it by reviewing all the personalities involved before going to the table. In this way you can take extra pains to avoid the confrontation if it seems that the mix of 4QB types involved is likely to tend this way.

Negotiation

The objective of a negotiation is agreement. Anyone who has listened to the leader of Northern Ireland's SDLP will hear John Hume use the words again and again, *we must have agreement.* It sounds so obvious that the wisdom of the sentiment may not always be apparent. If the three possible outcomes of division are domination, confrontation or negotiation, Hume's insistence on the third has special significance. Northern Ireland has suffered too long from domination and confrontation.

As I have already mentioned, the skill of negotiation is in finding the solution which gives *everyone* something of what they need, and psychometric assessment of the individuals involved will point you in the right direction. As long as High-Ds feel they have won a concession, High Is feel their point of view has been recognised, High Ss feel they have helped people, and High-Cs feel they have contributed to the mechanics of the solution, everyone will be happy.

FAIR AND WORKABLE

Any negotiated agreement must be:

FAIR
WORKABLE
NOT DAMAGING TO RELATIONSHIPS

Take the family planning a holiday. Mum, Dad and the kids all have different priorities. Mum could go to Cannes for sun and a level of sophistication, Dad could go to the west of Ireland for some peaceful fishing and the kids could go to Disneyland. It certainly seems fair but it is unlikely to be workable. The expense, the planning and the overall organisation would be horrendous. Further, relationships within the family would be likely to be damaged.

A fair agreement may not necessarily please everyone or anyone but if it is fair, it will survive scrutiny from an objective standpoint. So the interests of the parties have to be legitimate interests. Use your understanding of 4QB to ascertain what each party to the negotiation is likely to think of as 'fair' – and remember that   High-Ss will will be particularly sensitive to this aspect – and may also offer the best starting point for such an evaluation.

As regards workability, it is obvious that no agreement is worth the paper it's written on (if it *is* written!), unless it can be practically implemented. If there is a High-D participating in the negotiation, always listen to their views on this aspect...

As an example of the requirements of fairness, workability and non-damage to relationships, and of the difficulty sometimes of achieving them, consider the situation in Northern Ireland.

Part of the insoluble nature of Northern Irish politics is that some areas of division are totally irreconcilable. Historically the Unionist interests have been recognition of their British her itage, recognition of their religious heritage and political supremacy.

The first two are perfectly legitimate interests and part of Unionist fear is that in a re-united thirty-two county Ireland, these two legitimate interests might be in jeopardy. The third interest, though heartfelt by many, is not legitimate and cannot survive objective scrutiny as being fair. Orange marches which superficially are relatively innocuous if noisy parades are in essence an expression of this third interest, hence the ferocity of the interaction between the two communities during the marching season.

The Nationalist interests are recognition of their Irish her-itage and their religious heritage. The third interest is not as some believe, shared by all Nationalists – the wish for a re-united Ireland. For a significant proportion, equal rights and status within a UK administration will suffice. Historically, many Unionists have found neither acceptable. Hence the implacability of the slogans, *Ulster says No! No Surrender! Not an Inch!* or the almost mystical numerals, *1690!* The first step to negotiation in the province is to find areas where agreement is possible.

From a psychometric aspect, it is interesting to note that in the 1997 round of talks in Northern Ireland there were no High-Ds. Previously, the High-D Thatcher managed to contain the High-D Paisley not so much by dominating him but by neu-tralising him. However feisty the big man became, the Iron Lady was not one to be cowed by him. It was in the Major/Paisley exchanges where the sparks flew. The Paisley D type was always more likely to clash with the Major S type. The D cannot help being assertive and attempting to dominate. In the DISC/DEAA expression of 4QB the D stands for Driver and

Dominant. The S, on this occasion the Prime Minister of the UK, principled, decent and tolerant was hardly likely to accept a harangue from a minor figure from an outpost of the Kingdom.

In Jung's two hemispheres *Sensors* and *Intuitives*, Mowlam, Hume, Trimble and Adams all come from the same side. Whatever their differences, their *modus operandi* will be similar and if the language and process of negotiation are common to all, at least the train can leave the station. Where it terminates only history can show.

THE STRUCTURE OF NEGOTIATION

Just as it is important in selling to have a working, but flexible structure to the process, so it is important in negotiation to adopt a disciplined approach while retaining the flexibility to deal with the different personalities involved.

The standard first step in preparing for negotiation, as any negotiating manual will tell you, is to determine your 'L.E.M.' parameters:

L: What you would *like* to get out of the negotiation (the best-case scenario)

E: What you *expect* to get out of the negotiation

M: What you *must* get out of the negotiation (the minimum acceptable outcome)

Psychometric analysis of the individuals involved will help you to take this analysis one stage further, and analyse the L.E.M. parameter of *everyone else* at the negotiating table! If you already know the individuals concerned you may be able to include this in your preparatory analysis. Otherwise you will need to make some quick assessments as the negotiation gets under way, based on the personalities concerned, their initial stated positions, and, of course, the way that they modify their positions as the negotiation develops. High-D's will always overstate their position (starting at 'L' or better) and stick to this as long as they can hold out; High-Is will tend to look for an early compromise to keep everyone happy; High-Ss and High-Cs will probably start out quite close to their 'E' value, and seek to support this with rational argument.

Once you have assessed your L.E.M. and, if possible, that of your co-negotiators, you can plan the presentation of your case, and gear your strategy to the achievement of a universally acceptable solution.

The next step is to start negotiating – and it is here that the use of psychometrics can become critical. This is when it is vital to make the right impression and to establish an appropriate rapport with each individual involved in the discussions.

MAKING THE RIGHT CONNECTIONS

The rules are relatively straightforward. First of seek out a kindred spirit – one who shares the same personality profile as yourself – and try to use this connection to set up an immediate rapport.

Second, look out for types who hit your 'Blind Spots' as defined in earlier sections of this book – people with whom you are likely to struggle to find a natural connection. Special care should be taken to modify your approach to these individuals so that your own demeanour and disposition do not cause a negative reaction. Bend over backwards to accommodate their own style of negotiation, to avoid confrontation and ensure a constructive dialogue.

Finally, try to treat each personality type according to their particular needs. Thus:

High-Ds The High-D's nature is to assert, drive and control. They dislike waffle or uncertainty and tend to be impatient with preliminary courtesies. It is often best to play them at their own game. You might take the initiative and cut straight in with *'Why don't you begin by telling us precisely how you see the situation'*, or *'Tell us what you want'*. High-Ds have a tendency to bully but respect being stood up to, so it is wise to show resolve. Your message is *'I know precisely what I want from this meeting but tell me what you think first.'* High-Ds are interested in what you *can* do, so always back up a negative with a positive – *'There's no way I can discount the price but there might be some leeway on a service contract.'*

High-Is High-Is are more optimistic and gregarious. Handshaking, a back-slap, and humorous exchanges are common. They enjoy attention and recognition. They like the big picture and are bored easily with too much detail. Remember they respond strongly to praise – tell a High-I that his idea is a particularly good one and he'll eat from your hand. High-Is can be easily distracted, so if you need to keep him on-focus, check for agreements – *'You wanted the deadline set as the 25th, correct?'* or *'You'll contact your Head Office and report back by Friday, yes?'* High-Is take criticism badly so be wary of a cutting comment such as *'Would you please concentrate on the business in hand'*. High-Is are often too optimistic and over-willing to please, so beware of too rapidly made or extravagant promises.

High-Ss High-Ss are affable, amiable, loyal, steady, patient and concerned about human relationships. They also dislike change. They'll go the extra mile if they like you. So don't be brusque or smart with them. don't expect them to do anything *'behind the company's back'* or to be complicit in questionable practice. Even when disagreeing, acknowledge their views and humanity. If your proposal necessitates significant change, be prepared to sell the benefits of that change. Selling change should embrace benefits to people not just fiscal profits.

High-Cs   High-Cs are precise, cautious and disciplined and are painstaking in work which requires attention to detail. Don't expect them to respond to an emotional argument. They worry about their reputation and their career. Accuracy is important to them. Don't rush them. Don't try to gloss over figures. Be prepared to show proof. Avoid generalisations. When outlining a goal, be prepared to give a step by step explanation of how to reach it.

KICK THE EGO INTO TOUCH

It goes almost without saying that if you are to make full use of psychometric analysis in modifying your own behaviour in a given negotiation, you will need to lose your ego. Certainly, ego-based 'knee-jerk' reactions should be avoided at all costs.

Non-professional negotiators – the average citizen – may take offence when selling a house or a car if the the offer made is just too low. This results in the *I've never been so insulted in my life* stance. Experienced negotiators know its just a toe in the water by the other party to tease out where the seller's L.E.M. parameters are without revealing the buyer's L.E.M. range. Taking offence and storming off in high dudgeon is allowing the ego into the negotiation and is of no advantage to either buyer or seller.

Heavy negotiations are sometimes so fraught with egos and

emotions that indirect communication or a referee is necessary such as the Israeli/Palestinian peace talks at Camp David hosted by President Clinton. Divorce is another example where the parties are so emotionally tied up with the problem that they have to instruct lawyers to accomplish what is often a perfectly simple and fair arrangement. In the '97 Northern Ireland peace talks, feelings ran so high that the differing sides had to occupy separate rooms with the Secretary of State, Mo Mowlam, flitting from room to room. The participants do not have to like or respect each other. Hands need not be shaken. Pleasantries need not be exchanged but for any progress, it is essential to...

CONCENTRATE ON INTERESTS, NOT POSITIONS.

Concentrating on *positions* is all about ego. A successful negotiation must be *Fair, Workable and Not Damaging to Relationships.* Arguing positions is unfair, seldom workable and can damage relationships. Taking the ego out of negotiations can be particularly valuable when the psychometric mix is unfavourable. Assertives tend towards dominance. Buoyants wish to keep the negotiation moving and interesting. Carers seek harmony and the Detached check the details and small print. If the feelings of each side of a negotiation table are made clear and explicit then rational discussion is possible. As Roger Fisher and William Ury put it in their book, *Getting to Yes,* 'Freed from the burden of unexpressed emotions, people are more likely to work out a problem'.

During the marching season in Northern Ireland in 96 and 97, there was great ferocity at the Garvaghy Rd confrontation. The 'positions were a) the Orangemen claimed a historic right to march their traditional routes and b) the Nationalists saw it as an exercise in aggressive triumphalism.

Positions should always be subordinate to interests. A fine example of this principle was in January 9 when Mo Mowlam was determined to communicate with the terrorist godfathers.

Many of them were in jail in the Maze Prison. The Secretary of State for Northern Ireland could easily have taken the stance or *position* that Ministers of State of Her Majesty's Government do not go into prisons to speak with convicted terrorists. Who could have faulted her? But she disregarded *positions* and concentrated on *interests* and to her great credit went to the prison. One cannot envisage her polished and aristocratic predecessor, Patrick Mayhew, taking such a bold and enlightened step.

DON'T ACCUSE OTHERS, EXPLAIN HOW YOU PERCEIVE ACTIONS

It could be a worthwhile exercise to imagine the reactions of people to the following right and wrong statements in the light of their varying 4QB positions. For instance, how would a High-D say these and how would he react to hearing them. Knowing where you are in the 4QB analysis and where the person with whom you are negotiating is, can be a great aid to a successful outcome. It is not suggested that you should present your co-negotiator with a 16PF or a Myers-Briggs-type test before the interaction takes place, but careful observation and a keen ear will help establish probable reactions and approaches.

> **Wrong** – You are threatening me
> **Right** – I feel threatened
>
> **Wrong** – You are not listening to me
> **Right** – I feel I haven't made myself clear
>
> **Wrong** – You are putting pressure on me
> **Right** – I can't help feeling pressured
>
> **Wrong** – You are discriminating against me
> **Right** – I feel discriminated against

Wrong – You are ignoring me
Right – I feel ignored

Wrong – You disregard me
Right – I feel unimportant

Wrong – You don't like me
Right – Have I upset you?

The employee who says, *'You discriminate against me'*, may get the hostile response, *'Are you saying I'm a sexist/racist/bigot?'*

Whereas expressing how you feel rather than an accusation, *'I feel discriminated against'*, could be answered by *'I certainly don't discriminate against you'*, allowing the reply, *'I'm sure you don't consciously discriminate against me but I just can't help feeling I'm not treated equally'*. No-one can challenge your feelings. Anyone can challenge your accusations.

So by expressing your concerns wholly subjectively you cannot be wrong. You then have a basis for discussion to establish why interactive behaviour should implant such a concern. Expressing concerns or emotions as an accusation will evoke denial, anger, hostility and – the more accurate the accusation – the greater the vehemence. There is none so unforgiving as the wrongdoer.

Also the accusation can be entirely wrong. Fisher and Ury give the example of a foreman who sent for a specific employee every time he had a manpower shortage in another part of the assembly process. The employee felt discriminated against and victimised. It was only when the Trade Union representative challenged the foreman on the issue that the foreman explained that the man was the most reliable and diligent worker he had and chose him because of his competence. Your feelings cannot be wrong but your accusations can.

WIN-WIN

Most people are familiar with the concept of a 'Win-Win' situation. Ideally this should be the outcome of a negotiation. The four alternative outcomes are,

1. You win – I win   Best result
2. You win – I lose   Your victory
3. I win – You lose   My victory
4. I lose – You lose   Talks abandoned

The 'victory' situation is the result of any of the following,

Conceding	Attacking
Conforming	Dismissing
Pleading	Deception
Revealing	Insisting
Submitting	Presuming
Fear	Demanding

When both lose, the cause is usually ego and emotion.

Win-Win is the result of -

Making suggestions	Giving reasons
Stressing benefits	Summarising
Agreeing objectives	Testing understanding
Visualising	Defusing tensions
Supporting	Listening and reflecting
Understanding others' needs	Maximise interests
	Minimise positions
Using objective criteria	

It can readily be seen that the use of psychometrics provides direct assistance with almost all of the Win-Win processes. Three are particularly worthy of mention:

Testing understanding is important – checking that the

speaker and the listener are talking the same language and working on the same wave-length – and modifying your behaviour,if necessary, to achieve this.

Defusing tensions could be as simple as breaking for a cup of coffee when discussions gain some heat or choosing a very tranquil setting away from a war zone. As we have seen earlier in the book, psychometric analysis can provide an invaluable tool for anticipating this kind of negative tension, and taking preventative measures.

Listening and reflecting is important and is first cousin to **Testing understanding**. Sides can become entrenched by taking positions. Even with hostility there is no harm in comments such as, *So what you are saying is this... Is that correct? If I understand you correctly you are asking..... Just to clarify my thoughts, you wish to....* This process will help you to build on the rapport you have already established using the psychometric techniques referred to above; it will also help test your assumptions and assessments as you progress the negotiation.

Let us conclude with one of the ubiquitous slogans on managerial walls -

YOU DON'T PLAN TO FAIL, YOU FAIL TO PLAN

So whether you are involved in recruitment, an appraisal, a sale, a negotiation or a family situation, it is essential to have an understanding of yourself and the people with whom you will be dealing, and a plan based on a reasonable and logical format .... and may all situations be a Win-Win.

Epilogue

The mouth is the floodgate of the brain.

The study of psychometrics can be as serious as you wish it to be. It can also be be fascinating and fun. Understanding 4QB types will allow you to predict actions. People do run true to type. A relative who is a High-C had to drive some distance to his daughter's wedding. I called him shortly after his return. My wife, who can place the world on Jung's wheel after a few minutes conversation, was taking bets he would describe the journey. She, being a High-I, would naturally enthuse about the occasion, how lovely the bride was, the party atmosphere and all the sunny elements.

Her prediction was 100% correct. We were given a description of the prevailing weather, the road conditions and the duration of the drive. After some coaxing we found out that the bride was beautiful, which other relatives were there and the more frothy elements of the day.

Understanding 4QB makes you more tolerant, more perceptive, less sweepingly judgemental and it makes you more self-aware. We can understand why we clash with other people's methods and why they might find our behaviour incompatible or irritating.

Although this book will give you a reasonably clear indication of your personality preferences, you may wish to place yourself more precisely on the psychometric map, in which case contact the British Psychological Society or one of the major test publishers.

Index